THE S

SEA HARRIER   FRONT LINE

THE SHARP END
NEIL MERCER

714

715

Neil Mercer

THE SHARP END

SEA HARRIER   FRONT LINE

Airlife
England

This book is for my son Joseph with love and apologies for enforced absence due to career circumstances.

Photography

To complete the majority of the imagery for this book, Mr Harry Collins of Nikon (UK) Ltd kindly loaned me the Nikon F90 series of cameras and lenses. In the demanding cockpit, air-to-air and flight-deck environments the equipment performed faultlessly, and the photographs in this book reflect the versatility and quality of the Nikon F90. I am very grateful for the chance to use such excellent equipment for this project. Unless otherwise individually credited, all photography is by the author. Imagery marked 'CC' is MoD Crown Copyright, reproduced with permission of the Controller of HMSO.

Copyright © 1995 by Neil Mercer

First published in the UK in 1995 by Airlife Publishing Ltd

British Library Cataloguing in Publication Data
A catalogue record for this book is available from the British Library

ISBN 1 85310 544 9

Printed in Singapore by Kyodo Printing Co. (S'pore) Pte. Ltd.

Airlife Publishing Ltd

101 Longden Road, Shrewsbury SY3 9EB, England

Acknowledgements

I am indebted to the Commanding Officer of 899 NAS, Lt-Cdr Simon Hargreaves RN and his squadron for allowing me unique flying opportunities with the FA 2 OEU. Without these sorties and the help of my boss, Lt Pete 'Freddie' Smith RN, the project would not have come to fruition. Many thanks.

My brother Sam the Man dealt with the computer side, and would have been of more assistance apart from changes to my holiday plans by the Royal Navy. Sorry about Toulon – a large curry and a Holstein Pils please!

Phil Boyden at BAe provided excellent photographs from his superb collection.

CCAEA Brian Johnstone MBE kindly made available the information for the airframe listings at the annex – the most accurate available.

POAEM(M) Steve Titheridge had the perseverance to read the proofs when mine had run out!

Additionally, the following people were very kind to assist:

HMS *Invincible*:	LA(PHOT) Dave Trish.	Lt Simon Sparkes RN.
	LA(PHOT) Colin Burden.	LA(PHOT) 'Wolfie' Wilkinson.
	PO(AH) P. Devereux.	PO(AH) 'Bungy' Williams(!)
800 NAS:	Lt Roger Colquhoun RN.	Lt-Cdr Ewan Kelbie RN.
NFSF(FW):	Lt-Cdr T. Mannion RN.	Lt-Cdr Dave Baddams RN.
899 NAS:	Lt-Cdr Tim Eastaugh RN.	Lt Andy Davis RN.
	Lt Frank Hopps RN.	Lt Paul Stone RN.
	Lt Adrian Orchard RN.	Lt Lawler RN.
	Lt Pete 'Whizzer' Wilson RN.	CPO Jim Saywell (Sidewinder!)
	Lt Jack London RN.	Lt-Cdr M. Boast RN.
814 NAS	Lt P. Hannigan RN.	Lt J. Taylor RN.
	Lt J. Ford RN	Lt J. Powell RN.
849 'A' Flt	Lt P. Allen RN.	Lt R. Deverson RN.
BAe Dunsfold:	Phil Boyden.	Rod Frederiksen.

HALF TITLE: Specially marked 'The Sharp End' for this project, the Falklands veteran 714/XZ457 flown by Lt-Cdr Tim Eastaugh is seen outbound for the first deck landing of the type on board HMS *Invincible*.

CONTENTS

As all remaining examples of the Sea Harrier will be converted to the upgraded FA 2, the FRS 1 will never be seen in any museum. The characteristic pointed nose-cone and fine lines of the FRS 1 are demonstrated in the turn by 801 NAS during station-keeping with a Hercules tanker of 57 Sqn RAF Lyneham.

Undoubtedly the most capable air defence fighter in the UK armoury, the FA 2 mixes the traditional versatility of the combat proven FRS 1 with the deadly effectiveness of the Blue Vixen/AMRAAM combination. working from the Royal Navy's aircraft carriers as a fully integrated weapons system providing true maritime air defence and area denial capabilities.

FOREWORD

By Commander Nigel 'Sharkey' Ward DSC, AFC, RN

Commander Nigel 'Sharkey' Ward DSC, AFC is the highly experienced former Phantom pilot who was responsible for the introduction of the Sea Harrier to Royal Navy service, first commanding the 700L Intensive Flying Training Unit and then serving with distinction as CO of 801 NAS during the Falklands Conflict of 1982. Awarded the Distinguished Service Cross and Air Force Cross for his leadership and bravery, destroying three enemy aircraft in the South Atlantic, he is widely recognised as 'Mr Sea Harrier' and is seen here in this early photograph flying his personal aircraft. *(Phil Boyden BAe)*

I feel extremely privileged to be given the opportunity to write the foreword to this outstanding pictorial essay on Sea Harrier in the Front Line. Neil Mercer has created a showpiece of photographic journalism. He has combined his flair for capturing events on film with that rare ability to get across to his readers the feeling of professionalism and excitement that is the continuing hallmark of the Royal Navy Fleet Air Arm at sea.

When I spoke recently to the Flag Officer Naval Air, Rear-Admiral Ian Garnett, he told me with obvious pride and satisfaction of the impressive operational achievements of the men and machines of the Sea Harrier world in their United Nations support duties in the skies over Bosnia Hertzegoveha. As we did in the past, the Sea Harrier team is again satisfying the Government's urgent need to be able to deploy effective air power in hostile, foreign airspace. It is conducting highly reliable and successful operational missions in an 'inaccessible theatre' even when other, land-based air forces of NATO have been grounded by adverse weather conditions.

Just how 'inaccessible' is Bosnia Hertzegovena? It is less than one thousand miles from London. It is surrounded by the European countries of NATO and the European Union. It is not eight thousand miles away as are the Falkland Islands. Yet in spite of its proximity to our shores and to the territories of our Allies, the Tactical Air Support and Reconnaissance tasking of British Military Aviation resources over Bosnia has again fallen to the Royal Navy Carriers and Air Groups.

This Fleet Air Arm versatility has been the tradition of British Defence since the end of World War II: effective and rapid response to the nation's need conducted in an efficient manner.

I am therefore delighted that Neil Mercer has succeeded so well in documenting the recent, relatively unsung operational achievements of the men and machines that make up the world of Royal Naval Fixed-Wing Aviation and that provide Britain with effective, deployable air power. As he so rightly says, the new Sea Harrier FA 2 is the most potent and capable air defence vehicle in the United Kingdom inventory. It is maintained and supported to perfection by professionals. It is flown by professionals.

In days gone by I was extremely proud of my Sea Harrier team. The 'new look' Sea Harrier world as presented by Neil Mercer fills me with equal pride and optimism.

Well done, Sea Harrier!

Sharkey Ward

DSC, AFC

Flying in extreme close formation, around five feet from the wingtips of the photo chase Hawk, two aircraft of 899 NAS FA2 Operational Evaluation Unit head south over Swanage in Dorset, outbound to join HMS *Invincible* steaming off the Isle of Wight, June 1994.

The tripartite agreement of 1962 was negotiated to continue the P1127 development programme, with particular bias towards a Fighter Ground-Attack airframe. The result, named the Kestrel after the common European falcon, was granted a release for service flying in 1964 and amassed over 650 flying hours during successful evaluation in 1965. One of the nine original Kestrels is seen here during the evaluation period marked with the special tripartite roundels, accompanied by a Hunter chase. *(BAe)*

GENESIS – SEA HARRIER AND CARRIER DEVELOPMENT

The Sea Harrier is a modern success story for the Royal Navy, combining performance and versatility with the cost-effectiveness that must be the hallmark of any weapons system in the current financial climate. Development and eventual success have followed a tortuous path to fruition, with many political obstacles to overcome at every step, and it is no surprise to discover that the ship-platforms the aircraft operate from have a similar chequered history.

The story of the Sea Harrier really begins with the forward-thinking planners of the Hawker company, who in 1959 proposed the concept of operating VSTOL aircraft in the maritime environment. Under development at this time was the BE 53/2 project of Bristol Aero Engines, incorporating a proposal from the French engineer Michel Wibault of a conventional turbofan which discharged through nozzles, which in turn could be moved through an arc of approximately one hundred degrees to vector the thrust. This revolutionary concept was a breakthrough when compared to the deflection devices previously tested, and resulted in the Pegasus 1 which first ran at 10,000lb thrust in September 1959. Funded initially by the company due to the foresight of the chairman, Sir Reginald Smith, the remaining seventy-five per cent balance was eventually met by the US Mutual Weapons Development Program. This engine was further refined after the decision to use HP bleed air for aircraft reaction controls, and with modifications was finally cleared for flight at 11,000lbs thrust.

Powered by the Pegasus 2, the prototype VSTOL P1127 aircraft first flew in 1960, the project only attracting passing interest from the three armed services, although the government of the day heavily invested in research contracts with Hawker. However, after the prototype satisfied the specifications of NATO Basic Military Requirement No 3, this vague interest became more focused, with the Royal Navy and RAF being advised by the Air Ministry to study the subject of a common aircraft requirement for the type. Differences became apparent during this project, with the RAF favouring a supersonic ground-attack variant, and the RN preferring an air-superiority optimised catapult-launched fighter. The design team spent eighteen months attempting to amalgamate the two roles, but the final result proved unacceptable to either and the RN lost interest, subsequently purchasing the McDonnell F4K Phantom. The RAF, who continued to complete feasibility studies on both the supersonic P1154 and the subsonic P1127, finally had the decision made for them when the Labour government of 1965 cancelled the P1154 but allowed immediate progress on the P1127. A tripartite agreement of 1962 between the US, Britain and Germany continued the development of the P1127 which culminated in the Kestrel. The latest Pegasus 3 producing 15,000lbs thrust was fitted, with the Kestrel proving a success during evaluation, particularly in the US where the US Marine Corps immediately realised what the aircraft could contribute to their concept of independent autonomous amphibious operations.

In addition to the joint project evaluating possible commonalities for the VSTOL aircraft, the Royal Navy were given the first taste of these capabilities at sea, when the Hawker chief test pilot Bill Bedford flew a P1127 prototype out to HMS *Ark Royal* in Lyme Bay on 8 February 1963. Both he and the second test pilot Hugh Merewether had no experience of operating from aircraft carriers, yet they had little difficulty operating in the shipborne environment throughout the week of trials. At the time few people in the RN realised the significance of these trials, mainly because they were regarded as a novelty and of little import to the sizeable fixed-wing lobby within the service.

In 1965 the RAF requirement for a Kestrel type fighter on the front line (particularly in Germany where the VSTOL advantages of the type were unique) was finally answered. A ninety per cent redesign of the Kestrel, coupled with an uprated Pegasus of 19,000lbs thrust and the avionics suite of the cancelled P1154, produced the Harrier. Entering service with the RAF in 1969, a

succession of upgrades in powerplant and avionics have contributed to make the RAF Harrier a capable ground-attack aircraft, protecting NATO's flank where reaction time remains of the essence.

After the failure of the VSTOL project with the RAF in 1963, the RN had continued with conventional fixed-wing procurement, purchasing the Phantom for use on board HMS *Ark Royal* and logically for her proposed replacement, the planned 50,000-tonne CVA-01 carrier. Unfortunately in 1966, as a result of RAF insistence that the service could provide air cover to any theatre in a world, a change in defence policy brought the cancellation of the project. This devastating decision for the RN, taken inexplicably just as it had acquired the most powerful warship that it ever possessed (*Ark Royal*), left the Fleet Air Arm with excellent aircraft but a small fleet of ageing aircraft carriers whose demise in the early 1970s effectively ended any fixed-wing ambitions. Ironically the Phantom and Buccaneer aircraft went to the RAF, who put the types to good use in the maritime role.

Project studies for the RN in the 1960s had produced the concept of the light anti-submarine cruiser, able to carry ASW helicopters in the large numbers necessary to render them effective in protecting US aircraft carriers resupplying the NATO northern flank. This idea surfaced in the hostile procurement environment when 'aircraft carrier' was still a politically sensitive word, and although Naval departments were aware that VSTOL aircraft could operate from these platforms, this capability was kept quiet. Instead, the politically neutral yet transparent term 'through-deck cruiser' described the class of ship, which finally became reality with the ordering of HMS *Invincible* on 17 April 1973. As the realisation dawned yet again, that the RAF/NATO air umbrella could not provide air support worldwide, the class of ship became known for the task that they had been designed to do – carry aircraft. The design successfully merged the two lines of carrier development – the ASW carrier and the VSTOL concept. In retrospect, the problems over the categorisation of the class of ship appear over-emphasised, but it is worth considering that subterfuge necessarily extended to designing a particularly imposing superstructure to fool the uninitiated, and also to naming the first carrier after a cruiser (the previous *Invincible* having been sunk at the battle of Jutland in 1916). When the situation eased, the other two ships in the class could be more traditionally named.

In 1971 No 1 Sqn RAF deployed to HMS *Eagle* in squadron strength, exercising the Harrier GRI in the deployment of VSTOL aircraft to RN helicopter carriers in emergency. The lessons of this successful experiment were not lost on the RN, especially as fixed-wing operations had previously been considered terminated with the cancellation of CVA-01 and the loss of conventional aircraft. Initially discreet enquiries were made with very limited funding to procure a navalised variant of the Harrier optimised for use at sea, but in response to increasingly confident and specific demand from the RN the projected Sea Harrier began to take shape. Under the supervision of Dr John Fozard, the Chief Designer, the planning continued apace until ready for submission to Parliament for assent. On the actual day the proposal was due to be debated, more serious matters intervened thus depriving the team the clearance to proceed.

It was not until May 1975 that a fixed-price contract for twenty-four Sea Harrier aircraft was approved. Navalisation of the basic Harrier was intended to retain all the integral advantages of the design, optimised for easy maintainer access and equipped for rough self-sufficient tasks with low-pressure tyres and internal starting. In view of the aircraft's unique flight envelope, the latest Martin-Baker Mk 10 ejection seat was fitted to the cockpit, which had itself been raised eleven inches to improve visibility. Further changes implemented by the design team included the replacement of seven magnesium components in the airframe/engine to lessen corrosion in the maritime environment, increased tailplane travel and more power to the wingtip reaction controls, to give more roll authority in the hover alongside ships. The Air Intercept radar fitted to the nose of the new aircraft was derived from the Ferranti Sea Spray, conceived for the Lynx helicopter and initially designed for use in conjunction with the Sea Skua anti-shipping missile. The conversion was completed with the use of the Pegasus 104 producing 21,500lb thrust, with the finished product only weighing one hundred pounds more – an exceptional achievement. After the complete range of equipment intended for the new Harrier had been test-flown in three specially converted Hunters, the first Sea Harrier took to the air on 9 January 1978, flown by Chief Test Pilot John Farley, with a short and uneventful flight signalling the beginning of a new era for the Fleet Air Arm.

Simultaneously, work continued apace at Vickers Shipbuilding on HMS *Invincible*, which was launched on 3 May 1977 by HM the Queen. As with all first of class, delays were experienced in manufacture, although these were partly because these ships were the first capital ships to be built in Britain since the Second World War. The second and third hulls were ordered respectively in 1976 and 1978, to be named *Illustrious* and *Ark Royal* after two of the Royal Navy's most famous ships. Displacing 19,500 tonnes, HMS *Invincible* was accepted from the shipbuilder on 19 March 1980 and was rapidly set to work by the RN, being declared operationally ready in June of the following year. Driven by four Rolls-Royce Olympus TM3B gas turbine engines developing 11,200 shaft horsepower, the class made twenty-eight knots during sea trials and showed excellent sea-keeping qualities.

In May 1979 the first Sea Harrier was handed over to the Royal Navy, who re-formed the traditional 700 Naval Trials Squadron and tasked A Flight with the Intensive Flying Trials prior to front line service. Under the expert eye of a highly experienced ex-Phantom pilot, Lt-Cdr Nigel 'Sharkey' Ward, the Sea Harrier became the safest aircraft ever introduced to the Royal Navy, with its operational parameters being continuously re-evaluated as more and more of the remarkable qualities of the aircraft became apparent. By the time the front line 800 and 801 Naval air squadrons were commissioned in 1980, the type had established a clear reputation for reliability and availability, producing convincing results whether tasked for air intercepts, ship attack or reconnaissance. When the trials had been successfully completed the IFTU was disbanded, to be immediately re-formed as 899 Naval Air Squadron, tasked as the parent shore-based unit for training and supporting the two front line squadrons as required.

Sea Harrier and operating platform first met in November 1978, when the prototype landed on board HMS *Hermes*, but the aircraft finally went to sea proper when 801 NAS embarked to HMS *Invincible* to form the strike element of the Carrier Air Group (CAG). Tasked to take part in the joint exercise 'Ocean Venture', the aircraft soon demonstrated to the Americans the advantages of subsonic highly manoeuvrable VSTOL at sea, with the ship also providing top quality anti-submarine cover for the US aircraft carrier as originally designed. Availability for all sorties was excellent due to good serviceability, a trait that rapidly became the aircraft's hallmark, and the early realistic introduction of the type to sea stood the Royal Navy in good stead during the following year.

HMS *Invincible* had meanwhile built up a considerable amount of affection as the Royal Navy's only capital ship for some time before the appearance of the other two vessels, and so it was to vociferous public concern that the proposed sale to Australia was announced in 1981. Arguably motivated by sound reasoning, as

mistakes made during her build had been rectified in the other two ships, the concern hinged mainly on the appearance, that no sooner did the RN grow larger again than it was cut. Financially the Australians would be obtaining an excellent deal, as the ship which cost approximately £200 million to manufacture was available for £150 million, although an order for Sea Harriers was also expected. Initially keen, the Australian government then decided to run down the Australian FAA, which produced an influx of skilled aircrew to the British FAA but effectively ruled out the sale. Just as this was becoming a problem for both governments the Falkland Islands crisis intervened, solving the matter and inadvertently providing the Sea Harrier with the ultimate opportunity to confound the critics.

Deploying south with the Task Force, rapidly assembled after the personal intervention of the First Sea Lord to the Prime Minister, as many Sea Harriers as possible were taken by the Royal Navy who had suddenly appreciated their importance in a theatre of war eight thousand miles away. The out-of-area task again illustrated the folly of the argument, volunteered by the RAF, that they could provide air cover to any hot spot, and indicated once and for all that the Royal Navy must be able to conduct independent operations wherever required in the world.

Armed at the last possible moment with the latest Sidewinder missile from the US, the AIM-9L, the combination of aircraft and missile proved deadly to the Argentine Air Force. Flown by many of the highly experienced pilots who had introduced the aircraft to service, the Sea Harrier became known as the 'Black Death' to the Argentinians, who despite fighting bravely suffered heavy losses. The ground-attack RAF Harrier GR3 also fought from the carriers, proving the concept of VSTOL air operations in independent amphibious operations. HMS *Invincible* remained at sea for 166 days during the conflict, establishing a new world record for continuous carrier operations, and her jets remained serviceable for ninety-five per cent of this period. Forced to fight a war in a narrow inlet instead of the open sea, the Royal Navy lost one ship for every four enemy aircraft, and it is certain that without the Sea Harrier the conflict would not have had a successful outcome. No aircraft were lost in air combat, although several were destroyed by enemy action or the appalling weather conditions prevalent in the South Atlantic, and the Task Force returned to the UK, triumphant but with many lessons to be absorbed. The First Sea Lord, Admiral Sir Henry Leach, later said 'Without the Sea Harrier there would have been no Task Force' – vindication indeed for the fixed-wing Fleet Air Arm.

Attrition replacements for the aircraft lost in the Falklands were ordered from British Aerospace in 1983, and particular limitations of the aircraft highlighted by experience in action were studied. A staff target for an airframe mid-life update was identified in late 1982, designed to rectify the most obvious operational shortcoming in radar performance, manifested by the inability of the radar when deployed at high level to 'look down' and see a fast-moving target at low-level against ground clutter.

The Sea Harrier FA 2 is the result of these studies, and can be fairly described as a quantum leap from the previous aircraft, particularly with the Ferranti Blue Vixen pulse-Doppler multi-mode radar and the capability to carry the Hughes AIM 120B Advanced Medium-Range Air-to-Air Missile. Unique in being the first aircraft and radar in history to be designed to interface with a missile system, the awesome capability of the Blue Vixen radar combined with AMRAAM means that for the first time the Fleet Air Arm has moved into the Beyond Visual Range (BVR) area, a significant advantage at sea where the threat grows ever more

---

sophisticated. The AMRAAM alone completely redefines the concept of air combat with its exceptional range and advanced avionics, utilising target information from the Blue Vixen en route as mid-course guidance and switching to active homing in the terminal guidance phase. The radar designates targets in order of greatest threat closure and utilises automatic scheduling between medium and high PRF rates, while the Track While Scan (TWS) mode allows engagement to take place without alerting the target of radar lock, allowing the aircraft to launch four missiles and simultaneously track them all to separate targets. Additionally fitted with a digital database for rapid transfer of target information to the missile and enhanced software for bomb delivery, the aircraft retains a true multi-role capability, able to fulfil a number of separate specialised missions with the traditional Sea Harrier advantages of reliability, flexibility and rapid mission change as required by the command.

During the development of the FA 2 the original Sea Harrier FRS 1 has continued to give sterling service to the Royal Navy, both in the role of the Maritime Airborne Intercept/Fleet Fighter and in the secondary reconnaissance task. The Invincible class often operate in Norway in support of the Royal Marines, defending the Northern Flank as part of the UK commitment to the NATO alliance, and this deployment often requires the exercise of the type's primary role – rapid launch of aircraft to intercept maritime intruder aircraft. The Sea Harrier can be off the deck from alert in two minutes, with the ship not required to make any changes to course and speed, and despite the gentle thaw in relations between east and west due to the inevitable economic collapse of the Warsaw Pact, a high state of vigilance is maintained.

The carriers *Invincible* and *Ark Royal* have since been deployed to the messy conflict in the former Bosnia-Hertzegovena, where continuous Combat Air Patrols are flown in conjunction with the RAF to ensure the safety of British forces on the ground. The reconnaissance camera in the nose has also proved invaluable, particularly in revealing troop dispositions to the United Nations forces and in the monitoring of ceasefires. The late flowering of the reconnaissance role for the aircraft, although used in the South Atlantic in 1982, has earned great praise from the United Nations, who have particularly commented on the high serviceability achieved and the reliability of the system. The Sea Harrier has always delivered when required to do so, and will undoubtedly continue to do so in the Adriatic or any other theatre of operations.

First flown on 19 September 1988, the FA 2 aircraft is coming into service late due to development delays and uncertainty over finance, but the Operational Evaluation Unit has already been formed as a subsidiary of 899 NAS headquarters squadron, introducing the jet to the Royal Navy prior to full front line service by March 1995. The first jet was delivered to the Royal Navy in 1993 after CA release from Boscombe Down in 1990, and the OEU have immediately embarked on a succession of trials to assess the air-to-air capability when compared to the FRS 1. The fixed-price contract for the aircraft has resulted in a fairly basic aircraft which still requires some work and modification, particularly with the Vertical Speed Indicator pitot system moved from the nose and the Head-Up Display (HUD), but initial experience both ashore and afloat is proving that the fighter is what the Fleet Air Arm wants into the 21st Century. Already forming a third of the strength of 899 NAS, the new aircraft is supplied at the rate of around one every six weeks, re-equipping 801 NAS on their return from the Adriatic in 1994 and leaving 800 NAS the last squadron to operate the FRS 1 over Bosnia on 'Deny Flight' operations until the last FRS 1 will go for conversion.

Future planning for ships and aircraft requirements are proceeding at present, including the very promising concept of the Shipborne Containerised Air Defence System (SCADS) which containerises all the essential requirements of the modern warship, and be very quickly attached to any commercial container ship in the event that other assets would have to be deployed elsewhere. The unit could provide 30 days autonomous unreplenished air defence cover and protect itself with vertical launch Seawolf point-defence weapons, similar to those fitted to the 'Fort' class of replenishment ships. This concept utilises the unique advantages of the Harrier and combines affordability with versatility, critical as financial constraints will continue to dictate and regulate procurement in the foreseeable future.

From this abbreviated history it becomes rapidly apparent that rarely have two weapons systems become such hostages to the ebb and flow of political fortunes. Time and again the Royal Navy and Fleet Air Arm have been required to complete tasks allocated with less than ideal equipment, due to flaws in theory and equipment, and the fact that they have always done so is a tribute to the men and the spirit of the Senior Service. It is to be hoped that the hard-won lessons of 1982 and the permanent lessons of the past will be taken into account by the procurement executive of the future. In the Sea Harrier FA 2 and the Invincible class aircraft carriers, the Royal Navy has finally obtained some of the equipment that it deserves, and we may be sure that the Sea Harrier and the Fleet Air Arm will continue to protect British interests worldwide whenever called upon to do so.

On 20 August 1978 the Royal Navy finally
re-entered the fixed-wing field, when John
Farley flew the first production Sea Harrier
XZ450 on its maiden flight from BAe
Dunsfold. During a 35-minute flight the
aircraft was put through a basic selection
of VSTOL transitions and recoveries
without problem, in a sortie described by
the Chief Test Pilot as 'uneventful'. *(BAe)*

The Invincible class was designed to carry sufficient heavy ASW helicopters to give 24-hour 'ripple' cover to American aircraft carriers as required. The Sea King, although an old airframe, has received successive updates of acoustic and related equipment up to Mk 6 standard, and in the right conditions is a competent submarine killer, armed with depth-charges and homing torpedoes. 814 NAS here conduct Quality and Assurance proof tests on the Mk 11 Mod 3 depth-charge off Portland, delivering the weapon then turning on a reciprocal heading to put the explosion behind the helicopter.

LEFT:
Converted from basic RN T8 airframes, the three Hunter T8(M) aircraft were used to flight test the entire range of operational equipment prior to fitting in the SHAR. First flown in 1978, two Hunters were allocated to 899 NAS as radar trainers after completion of these trials, flying for many years as an invaluable part of the Blue Fox training package. However, no longer required after the FA 2 entered service in 1993, they were cannibalised for spares and now sit in the open at RNAS Yeovilton pending disposal. Often tasked to carry out secondary 'hack' duties, the first conversion aircraft 723/XL580 carries the author during a photographic sortie, shortly before retirement of the type.

BELOW:
Initially painted gloss navy-blue with white undersides, the paint scheme was rapidly toned down for the Falklands conflict, when experts from the Royal Aircraft Establishment at Farnborough advised a colour scheme to blend in with the operational environment of the Falkland Islands. Slight differences in grey occurred due to differing paint stocks on the ships, but the resulting paint scheme remained Extra-Dark Sea-Grey for the following twelve years until the role of the FA 2 dictated further change.
(Phil Boyden BAe)

801 NAS was commissioned on 26 February 1981, equipped with the full projected peacetime commitment of five aircraft. Allocated to HMS *Invincible*, the squadron rapidly attained all-weather operational capability, and is seen embarking to the ship for the first time. Of interest is the ship's ski-ramp, which at this time was still a gentle seven degree slope, and the lack of any point defence Close-In Weapons Systems (CIWS) prior to the sharp lessons of the Falklands War.
(Phil Boyden BAe)

The immediate requirement for fixed-wing assets generated by the Falklands produced a third operational fast jet Naval Air Squadron within two and a half weeks, achieved by rounding up aircrew from other appointments, expediting manufacturer deliveries of new airframes and available training assets. Commanded by Lt-Cdr Tim Gedge, 809 NAS obtained two pilots from the RAF with relevant experience, mustering eight aircraft to make the nine-hour flight down south. Before deploying on 30 April 1982, the unit undertook one photex on the 27th, and this remains the only time the squadron was photographed airborne. The fin badge, a phoenix rising from the flames, is displayed to advantage against the newly-painted grey tails of the aircraft.
(Phil Boyden BAe)

Primary role of the aircraft was to 'hack the shad', or destroy the long-range Maritime Patrol Aircraft reporting the position of any task force. The closest reality ever provided was in 1982 when the then Lt Simon Hargreaves was ordered to intercept the Argentinian Boeing 707 tracking the progress of the Task Force south. Although applicable rules of engagement precluded shootdown, a successful intercept was carried out and photographs taken by both sides. Russian Bear and Badger MPA were regularly encountered during NATO exercises in the 1980s, providing the normal cold war encounters and wary battle of wits. The huge Bear, audible for miles due to its contra-rotating propellers, dwarfs the intercepting SHAR from 800 NAS during such training in 1985. *(Rob Schwab)*

RIGHT:
Late in the service life of the FRS 1 came the confusing and unpleasant civil war in the former Yugoslavia, necessitating permanent aircraft carrier deployment to the Adriatic in support of 'Operation Deny Flight' and the British troops ashore. As only two aircraft carriers are in commission at any one time, this meant rotation in theatre six months about, handing over each March and August. During August 1994, HMS *Ark Royal* steams close in fog as the Sea Kings of 820 NAS ferry liaison teams, assist with the handover of responsibility to HMS *Invincible* off Gibraltar.

BELOW:
An important part of the 'Deny Flight' UN and NATO tasking has been reconnaissance of the warring factions, monitoring fighting, force dispositions and deterring the combatants from attacking the civilian populace with the rudimentary yet effective indigenous airpower. Although many specialist recce units are in theatre, the Sea Harrier has proved its worth at rapid off-the-deck reaction to the request of shore agencies, particularly when adverse weather sealed off Italian airbases. This reliability leads to much sea time for the British carriers, instilling confidence in the troops by being almost continually on station as a visible presence. The reconnaisance pair here pull G during a recce sortie over Bosnia-Hertzegovena in 1993, turning on to a patrol line over Modracko Jezero near Tuzla.

Additionally tasked with Close Air Support, under direction from a ground-based Forward Air Controller (FAC), the SHAR regularly flies over Bosnia armed with live 1,000lb bombs, indicated by the yellow band on the dull green casing slung underneath XZ498 over Split. The high-level bombing profile, commencing at 15,000ft with weapon release at 7,000 ft, is good enough to put a bomb in an individual house, accuracy essential in a 'dirty' war where collateral damage is twisted into propaganda.

Special markings on Royal Navy aircraft are rare, generally regarded as the province of the more junior RAF. However, in 1992 exceptional permission was granted for tail and nose markings to commemorate the 50th anniversary of 899 NAS. The three different types of aircraft operated by the squadron at that time are seen in immaculate formation, led by the T4(N) and followed respectively by the CO's FRS 1 and Hunter T8(M). This photograph is now history, as by 1995 all three types will have been converted or retired.

Early radar work required much singleton and formation target simulation, flown mainly by the Hunters of the Fleet Requirements and Direction Unit augmented occasionally with 899 NAS aircraft. A specially converted HS 125 was used as a test-bed, checking parameters and lock-up abilities at varying altitudes with single and multiple targets. Lt-Cdr David Morgan leads a four-ship calibration over the Bristol Channel on 21 March 1991.

After many delays and inevitable uncertainty, the FA 2 finally arrived at RNAS Yeovilton in September 1993. This historic wartime airfield, home of the fixed-wing Fleet Air Arm, has seen many types operated by the RN during fifty years as an active air station. Lt Adrian Orchard drops down over the field on a typically hazy June morning, short finals to land on runway 27 after a low-level radar elevation sortie with a T4(N) target.

Surrounded by the handling party after the first deck landing on board, the FA 2 is taxied forward to be parked. During the week-long trials programme the aircraft effectively demonstrated its advanced capability as advertised, also completing essential deck parking, hangar sizing and lift check movements. *(D. Coombs)*

Despite initial teething snags, experienced with any new high-tech introduction to service, early indications are that the aircraft has produced much happiness amongst the small SHAR fraternity. The OEU of 899 NAS were the first to receive two FA 2s, side numbers 723 and 724, prompting the inevitable jokes about the 'Historic Flight' jets on the Front Line. Somerset in June is the place to conduct photographic sorties, providing an impressive background near the old Roman town of Ilchester as one of the original OEU FA 2 jets orbits at low-level.

RIGHT:
After successful short embarkation to ships in UK waters, the decision was taken to send a larger detachment to sea in an operational environment for further evaluation. Led by the Commanding Officer of 899 NAS, the team of highly experienced aircrew brought four aircraft on to HMS *Invincible* as the ship deployed for the second time to the Adriatic.

BELOW:
Throughout September 1994 the four airframes were used intensively, first undertaking Combat Air Patrol (CAP) and ship attack training and then advancing the night qualifications of aircrew to give an all-weather capability prior to arrival on station. Once off the former Yugoslavia, normal recce sorties were flown armed with live weaponry, fully integrated with the FRS 1s of 800 NAS performing the same task.

ABOVE:
A baptism of fire in more ways than one, as one of the aircraft evaded a man-portable missile fired near the Bihac pocket, this successful deployment to *Invincible* proved the fighter in operational conditions, typified by this view of 7121/2/ZE696 over Sarajevo armed with live missiles. Educating the ship team and Carrier Air Group about the advanced aircraft to come, 800 NAS now look forward to re-equipping with the FA 2 on their return from Bosnia in March 1995.

LEFT:
The high humidity of the Adriatic is shown by the clouds forming in the air intakes of this aircraft, as it recovers from another sortie over Bosnia. Evident in this view are the live Sidewinder 9M missiles on underwing pylons, and the removal of the 30mm Aden cannon to minimise all-up weight.

THE SHIPS AND CARRIER AIR GROUP

Today the three Invincible class aircraft carriers are the Royal Navy's most prestigious surface assets, rotated in turn to leave two ships in commission at any one time. Attached to each commissioned unit is an associated Combat Air Group (CAG), comprising a rotary-wing element of one Sea King Anti-Submarine Warfare (ASW) squadron, a flight of 849 NAS Airborne Early Warning Sea Kings, and a fixed-wing Sea Harrier squadron. These aviation units are kept ashore at their respective air stations when the ship is alongside, embarking as required for aviation work-ups, exercises and deployments. Main roles of the ships remain as originally envisaged, being primarily an ASW operating base to protect USN carriers, secondly to provide organic air cover to the fleet, and thirdly to supply full flagship and Command services when required.

Carrier tasking after the Falklands conflict has generally been employed on large-scale military exercises out of area, working with foreign navies as part of the NATO alliance as well as frequent trips to Norway, practising the defence and resupply of the Northern Flank with the Sea King commando squadrons and the Royal Marines. Tasked in 1993 with the support of the United Nations operations in the former Yugoslavia, HMS *Invincible* and HMS *Ark Royal* have relieved each other every six months in the Adriatic, providing ASW cover as required and Sea Harrier close air support, combat air patrol and reconnaissance missions to support the United Nations Operation 'Deny Flight'. Successful completion of this tasking will indicate once again that the Royal Navy remains capable of protracted out-of-area power projection, as tasked by HM Government in the defence of British interests both in home waters and overseas.

After six months in the Adriatic, it is a pleasant sight to see the relief carrier appear over the horizon, and to witness the pained smiles of her crew at the numerous signs informing them of the large number of days they have on station before they will return. Taking part in the photex surrounding each handover, a Sea King of 820 NAS inadvertently becomes part of the overall picture, producing a rainbow during a low hover around the bows.

Extended sea time without shore support dictates a considerable amount of Replenishment At Sea (RAS), an area in which the Royal Navy traditionally excels. The art of station-keeping two large ships in close formation for long periods is extremely difficult, although long practice appears to indicate the contrary. Ships of the Royal Fleet Auxiliary supply the carriers with liquids (fuel, aviation spirit), solids (stores, food) and ammunition around every three days, as although *Invincible* has great range it is deemed advisable for task purposes to keep the tanks full at all times.

Displacing over 20,000 tonnes each, two aircraft carriers in close proximity are a truly impressive sight from the air. Large identification letters on the stern of each ship – known in deck parlance as ship's letter – show *Invincible* (right) and *Ark Royal* (left) off Gibraltar on hand-over day August 1993. Naturally many helicopters are up recording this rare meeting, resulting in a photographic version of Air Day!

Commitments to be the 'on-station carrier' are shared with the French and American assets occasionally in area, although the French have the luxury of the 'local' Navy base at Toulon, enabling them to be on standby whilst alongside. Normal notice for operations is 96 hours steaming time, curtailed to 48 hours in times of tension as requested by shore authorities. In an unusual meeting arranged for public relations purposes, *Invincible* turns sharply to port at around 25 knots from FNS *Clemenceau* after joint operations in theatre.

OPPOSITE:

In their primary role, the Sea Kings of 814 Naval Air Squadron practise Anti-Submarine Warfare on an opportunity basis, normally with UK/US submarines when available. Adriatic tasking has degraded ASW effectiveness in area, due to the lack of training opportunities and the lack of 'in contact' time, therefore regular short passages are taken out of area to retain effectiveness in this important field, practising 24-hour ripple flying for days at a time. Responsibility for personnel transfer, mail collection and VIPTAX (VIP transfer) rest firmly with the embarked ASW helicopters when ports of call are few and far between. The aircraft are stripped and converted to the Sea King Utility for these purposes, giving more internal capacity and greater lifting ability for VERTREP (Vertical replenishment by helicopter) tasking.

The Sea King Mk 6, with its new 'silent' intercom and improved sonics, is shortly to be retro-fitted with an emergency lubrication system for the main gearbox. Previously, several aircraft have dumped main gearbox oil within seconds, leaving little alternative but the controlled water landing and damage to a valuable aircraft. The emergency system will give the pilot vital extra minutes to recover to the ship's deck, hopefully considerably reducing the ever present nightmare of the ditching and inverted roll. Egression techniques are taught in the excellent 'dunker' at RNAS Yeovilton and are mandatory for all aircrew but only the foolhardy would willingly practice them for real. Lt David Bartlett of 814 NAS flies one of these aircraft back to the ship after a routine call to Gibraltar, the British colony forever associated with the Royal Navy and home of the industrial-strength hangover.

In the Falklands conflict, the Royal Navy were taught a sharp object lesson in the necessity of Airborne Early Warning (AEW) to detect fast-moving low-level targets. One ship was lost for every four Argentinian aircraft destroyed, an intolerable attrition rate against a third-rate air power even after analysis of the difficult predicament facing the warships. In typical British style, within eleven weeks this deficiency was rectified by mounting and integrating a Marconi Searchwater radar in an inflatable 'bag' on the starboard side of a Sea King, designated the AEW Mk 2A. Two aircraft of 849 'A' flight, call-signs Funnell One and Two, overfly HMS *Invincible* during a flypast farewell for the CO of the flight, Lt-Cdr Nick Funnell, on 13 September 1994.

OPPOSITE:
814 Naval Air Squadron is an affiliated 'Tiger' squadron, membership of which is limited to those NATO units featuring a tiger in the unit badge. Operational commitments precluded attendance to the 1995 'Tiger' meet, so in place an unusual colour scheme was specifically produced to be photographed then removed immediately, producing this unique shot as Captain Allen RCAF hovers very close to the photographic aircraft.

The first helicopter in the world to be used as an AEW platform, the introduction to service of the type has been a notable success. Supervised from the HQ of 849 NAS at RNAS Culdrose, 'A' and 'B' flights are embarked as required to provide fast warning of target course, speed, range and bearing via secure speech data links to the Ops team on the carrier. The AEW observer is highly trained on one of the most expensive courses in the Fleet Air Arm, skilled at controlling and vectoring fixed-wing assets to engage designated targets, which can be detected at ranges well in excess of 100 nautical miles. One pilot is assisted by the observer during critical flight phases, standing by to take manual throttle control in the event of an engine freeze or runaway. Here the three AEW Mk 2As of 849 'A' flight practice close formation in the Adriatic on 18 February 1995, a view enhanced by the perspective compression of the long lens on the Nikon F90.

OPPOSITE:
Entry to foreign naval ports normally calls for ceremonial duties of the highest level, with Toulon no exception as *Invincible* heads towards the famous dockyard in full 'Procedure Alpha'. The Alpha range shows off the embarked aircraft to advantage, and the officers line the superstructure with men fell in around the flight-deck. Drill Sea Dart missiles and the volunteer ships band complete the picture while the Alouette photographic aircraft circles on a cold but sunny French morning.

The long days after hand-over finally drag past giving way to Up Channel Night, the traditional Royal Navy way of celebrating the last night at sea after a long deployment. Many and lurid are the tales of what goes on after dark on this special evening, during which large quantities of alcohol are apparently mislaid on board. On an unseasonably good day in February, HMS *Invincible* returns to the familiar landmarks of Old Portsmouth, watched by long separated friends and families from the beach and the Round Tower. *(D. Coombs)*

ABOVE:
The fixed-wing CAG element invariably embark to the ship when steaming south of the Isle of Wight or in the South-West Approaches, both within easy reach of diversion airfields in case of problems. Individually completing the long finals circuit before selecting nozzles down, the aircraft begin to decelerate to the hover around four hundred yards aft, arriving alongside the designated landing area or 'spot' at the same speed as the ship.

LEFT:
After each deployment the ships undergo an extended maintenance period, known as a BAMP or Base Assisted Maintenance Period. Essential dockyard tasks are undertaken, including dry-docking for hull checking and cleaning, following which the ship is refloated and again sets to sea for Sea Acceptance Trials (SATs) on the marine and weapons systems. With these tests complete the CAG can again embark for the required aviation shakedown, training new joiners and exercising the ship back into routine.

The previously vast open space of the
flight-deck rapidly fills up as the
embarking FA 2s taxi forward before being
chain lashed securely to the deck
ringbolts. The five-ton deck tractors,
powered by the same engine as a London
Routemaster bus, await the pilots' exit
before moving the 'cabs' back to the deck
park in the background.

Routine joining administration complete, intensive flying is undertaken throughout aviation shakedown to re-establish professional expertise in one of the most dangerous and demanding disciplines in the world – operating from the flight-deck of an aircraft carrier under way. From the catering staff looking after the needs of the extra manpower, to the aircrew themselves, the whole ship begins to work once more as a team with the common aim of putting the Sea Harrier where it belongs, in the air in the maritime environment.

FLYING THE
SEA HARRIER

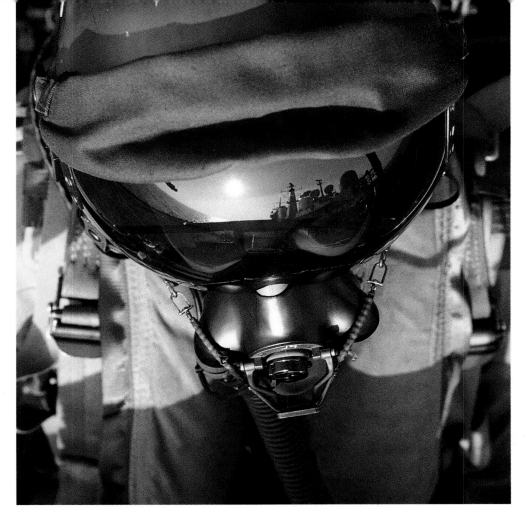

LEFT:
The single most important factor in the successful operation of the Sea Harrier is the pilot himself. In any single-seat fighter cockpit management is paramount, but in the most advanced fighter of its type this is taken for granted after one of the most intensive training programmes in existence. The island superstructure and the deck can be seen reflecting in the pilot's helmet visor as he completes pre-flight preparation for another 'Deny Flight' sortie over Bosnia.

BELOW:
SHAR aircrew mainly enter the training pipeline after being removed from the main helicopter pipeline at the end of EFT, progressing straight to the Tucano with 1 FTS RAF at Linton-on-Ouse. Further training with the Hawk follows, before finally arriving at 899 NAS to study VSTOL on the T4(N).

RIGHT:
Many promising aircrew are prevented from a chance to fly the Sea Harrier merely due to demographic factors, as the training pipeline can only accept about a dozen students per year to maintain a trickle of qualified aircrew to the front line. This anomaly is recognised by the RN, who provide a 'second chance' in the form of the SMAC 309 option, in which pilots are trained at RNAS Yeovilton in Hunters and Hawks after one or two tours as rotary-wing aircrew. A Hawk trainer leads out the seven Sea Harriers and four T4(N) trainers for the 50th Anniversary flypast of 899 NAS on 10 February 1992.

BELOW:
Initially produced to an RAF contract for a two-seat combat capable VSTOL trainer, the Pegasus 103-powered T4(N) weighs in at only 1,500lbs more than the SHAR. Cleared to fly from decks when required, the aircraft is an excellent trainer sharing almost identical handling characteristics as the single-seat, and is seen here on a low-level familiarisation trip over the M5.

After around nine months jet training the student finally reaches the last step before the front line – the busy line of 899 NAS. RNAS Yeovilton is currently the busiest airfield in Europe, handling thousands of movements every year, and apparent in this view is the tower of the Fleet Air Arm Memorial Church. Restored by appeal and re-consecrated as a tribute to all the members of the Fleet Air Arm who have given their lives whilst serving, the proceeds from this book and its predecessor *Fleet Air Arm* are contributing to the material upkeep of this beautiful and historic church.

The training pipeline is designed to reflect current front line philosophies as accurately as possible, necessitating a greater emphasis on reconnaissance as a direct result of the task in Bosnia. Target search sorties are undertaken and film processed as rapidly as possible for post-flight analysis and maximum training value. Full Image Movement Control should be set on the F95 camera of 716/XZ494 on a low recce sortie photographing the lighthouse on Start Point, Devon.

LEFT:
The air combat side of the SHAR syllabus is also not neglected, with basic radar work progressing to advanced tactics and engagement theory. Close formation, essential for pairs work and recovery through cloud is repeatedly exercised, normally with the instructor in the T4 and student in the single-seater. Displaying the specially painted anniversary tails, an FRS 1 tailchases the instructor's T4 during high G manoeuvring above the cloud layer.

BELOW:
General handling, learning to 'feel' how the aircraft responds to control inputs and responds in different flight configurations, gives the students an opportunity to see the local area from a new viewpoint. In the high workload environment of a Simulated Attack Profile (SAP), the aircraft weaves and twists at low-level in the turbulent coastline airflow.

Air-to-air refuelling has today assumed a dominant position in the operation of fighter aircraft, not only because fuel has always been a weapon in the air combat equation but because it has become a force extender, allowing long-range deployment of assets at extremely short notice. The fuel-critical Sea Harrier would be heavily reliant on AAR in any future conflict, demonstrated both by the fourteen refuelling couplings required to get the aircraft to the Falklands and the way SHARs are refuelled after launch over the Adriatic prior to heading inland for long-range tasks.

RIGHT:
Refuelling training exercises take place with both the slow Hercules and the faster Tristar to familiarise the student with the various types of approach required. Described as 'flying your left shoulder gently into the basket' the bolt-on refuelling probe needs accurate and sustained formation flying for fuel transfer, especially at slow speed with full flap down behind a Hercules. At the end of this tactical refuelling exercise, Lt Paul Simmonds-Short puts 711/ZE690 in close formation to give the tanker crew a good view of their satisfied customer.

48

The Operational Evaluation Unit for the FA 2 was formed on 1 June 1993 at Boscombe Down, with the first aircraft 723/ZD615 arriving on the 21st of the month and the second on 19 August. At this stage cockpit and radar capability assessments were carried out over the six-month stay at Boscombe, hampered slightly by the unfortunate loss of an FA 2 due to unrelated mechanical failure off Lundy Island. When delivered the aircraft could only be flown Visual Flight Rules (VFR) due to the unsolved ASI problem, but as work continued the clearances were progressed until in January 1994 the Unit transferred to Yeovilton. Now comprising a third of 899 NAS strength, progress continues to be made to prepare the aircraft for front line service, as the first jet 723/ZD615 overflies the squadron buildings and hardstanding after another radar trial assisting the Air Warfare Instructors course.

For twelve years after the Falklands War Extra-Dark Sea-Grey was the approved camouflage for the FRS 1, an accepted winner that did not require changing. However, as the FRS 2 evolved into the FA 2 and the role of the aircraft changed, it was perceived that a change would be necessary to reflect more emphasis in the air defence role. A paper submitted by the then Lt Henry Mitchell on his AWI course spelled out the reasons for change, suggestions that were adapted and resulted in the new light grey colour scheme. Significantly lower visibility ranges have been reported, with this photo clearly showing the differences in colouring at medium level.

899 NAS has now completely converted to the FA 2, with the remaining FRS 1s on the front line all due for replacement by March 1995. 801 NAS converted after returning to the UK in September 1994, leaving 800 NAS the last operator of the Blue Fox. FA 2s continue to dribble back from conversion at the rate of about one every six weeks from BAe Dunsfold, where they are test-flown by the civilian flight test pilots before collection. All remaining FRS 1s are to be converted, with an order placed for a further eighteen new-build airframes, the first of which (ZH796) has already begun manufacture. The T4(N) trainers will also be converted to T Mk 8 standard, fitted with a representative HUD, cockpit layout and navigation equipment.

OPPOSITE:
An astonishing photograph, taken by Lt Pete Wilson in some impossible position, shows the view in the cockpit of the FA 2 as though looking over his left shoulder in flight. The video head to record the HUD display can be seen projecting above the crash pad, whilst the position of the small panel in front of the control column illustrates vividly the major problem with the aircraft. During Carrier Controlled Approach to the ship, the stick is normally well forward, obscuring the essential Angle of Attack (AOA) dial in the centre of the panel. In the speed critical Sea Harrier this presents a major concern, as does the size and visibility of the remaining instrumentation on this panel. Although some of this information is duplicated in the HUD, the added unreliability of this system also causes concern, increasing the likelihood of the aircraft never receiving a complete night clearance for 'blue water' ops out of range of diversion airfields. This problem has already secured money for rectification, and is a good illustration of the task to be met by the OEU. The up-front control panel below the crash pad has received nothing but praise, combining with the Hands on Throttle and Stick (HOTAS) capability to produce a generally well designed ergonomic cockpit.
(Pete Wilson)

Typical radar sorties flown by the unit are composed of two FA 2 aggressors and one target T4(N), with the two fighters prosecuting the target as a pair for tactics formation. The trio take-off as a three ship vic from the wide main runway, and as the take-off proceeds interesting VSTOL characteristics manifest themselves in the way the aircraft behave. With a nod from the leader, throttles are pushed fully forwards accelerating the aircraft sharply at almost 1G down the runway. Below 140 knots the wing gives little lift, so when the leader decides to lift the nose at 130 knots he has to physically climb on the nozzles by angling them slightly downwards, causing the aircraft to literally leap off the runway and apparently decelerate momentarily before the nozzles rotate aft again and the aircraft picks up speed. Passing 180 knots the gear travels up and the immaculate formation blasts out of Yeovilton over the Somerset Levels en route to the Bristol Channel. The dissection of this phase of flight may seem unnecessarily clinical, but the real sensation from the 1G initial acceleration to the airborne transition is exhilarating and does not lose its attraction.

ABOVE:
The trend towards out of area employment for aircraft carriers will favour the versatile FA 2, which now puts the Fleet Air Arm on an equal footing with the rest of the world. The pilot now has a wealth of information at his fingertips, which if properly used should decrease the cockpit workload when compared with the FRS 1.

RIGHT:
On short finals to land on HMS *Invincible* in the Adriatic, the FA 2 HUD picture relays essential information to the pilot for recovery, easing the workload during the transition to the hover by additionally providing Jet Pipe Temperature (JPT) and water flow readings. The projected data in this photograph also shows the aircraft at 400 feet 150 knots with a JPT of 675 degrees and water selected.

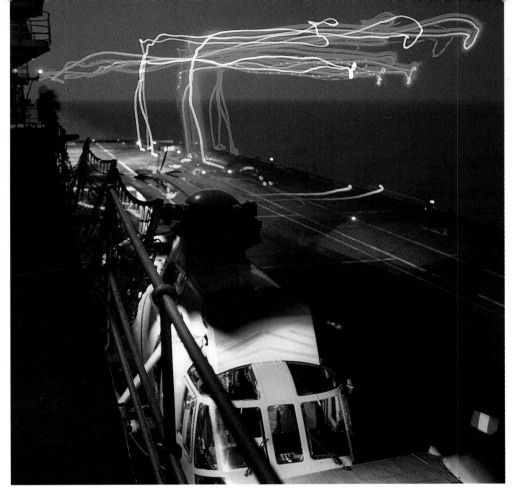

LEFT:
Approaching the ship, the pattern made by the nosewheel and anti-collision lights at night clearly shows the approach alongside the deck, before the standard transition across and descent to a positive landing. The approach and landing demand great pilot skill due to the lack of visual references and the little relative movement between them, commonly referred to as the 2-D effect. *(Colin Burden)*

BELOW:
At the end of the FRS 1's career, 800 NAS has progressed night flying to its ultimate end – no deck floodlighting on take-off and only the Deck Approach Position System (DAPS) above Flight Control (FlyCo) and faint runway lights on recovery. Precautions are taken to preserve aircrew night vision, so a photograph at night can only be taken at the end of flying stations, and even then only with great difficulty. The deck at night is even more dangerous than by day, and it is a tribute to the professionalism of the aircraft handling branch that accidents are few and far between.

FIGHTING
THE
AIRCRAFT

As previously discussed, the initial projected role of the Sea Harrier was to intercept and destroy Maritime Patrol Aircraft shadowing any task force, a threat effectively honed by the Warsaw Pact during many years of practice. Armed with deadly very large stand-off anti-shipping missiles such as 'Kitchen' and 'Kelt', capable of long-range launch and attack profiles best described as very unpleasant, this form of attack could be countered by early interception and termination of the missile-carrying bombers. This excellent and very rare colour photograph by Lt Rob Schwab of 800 NAS shows a Badger intercept during Fleet Exercises off Norway in 1986. *(Rob Schwab)*

Before launch with live or acquisition training rounds, a test is carried out with an infra-red source on deck to check coolant flow and ensure the seeker head has full and free movement. Known as the 'growl' check after the audio signal the missile gives to the pilot when it sights a heat source, a supervisory maintainer listens for the growl as the source is moved around at the front of the missile, only with the acquisition weapon pressing the 'accept' switch to check the 'chirp' response indicating lock-on.

RIGHT:
Before the widescale introduction of head-on Beyond Visual Range (BVR) missile technology into the air combat equation, the most effective method of destroying another fighter was the Sidewinder missile. Combat proven all over the world and now improved to 9M standard, this heat-seeking missile proved deadly with the Sea Harrier during the Falklands War. Supplied at the last minute with the latest version of the weapon by the Americans (the 9L), the combination of top quality pilots and good environmental conditions for the missile destroyed twenty-four Argentinian aircraft without loss in air combat. The cold background of the Islands and the South Atlantic highlighted the jetpipes of the Mirage and Skyhawk like the sun to the nitrogen-cooled seeker head of the missile, an advantage that made the SHAR so lethal it was nicknamed 'The Black Death' by its opponents.

PREVIOUS PAGE:
Live missiles are rarely fired, both because most training profiles can be flown and assessed up to launch without release, and the ever present spectre of cost. When fired the delivery profile is deliberately designed for a 'hard shot', to explore some aspect of the weapon parameters that may not have been fully tested. Live firing for the SHAR takes place under the auspices of the RAF Strike Command Air-to-Air Missile Establishment (STCAAME) at RAF Valley in North Wales, with the range and launch area over Cardigan Bay. Outbound for the second live firing on the Air Warfare Instructors course, Lt Frank Hopps flies past the lighthouse on Bardsey Island at low-level with the live missile on the starboard outer pylon.

ABOVE:
This particular profile requires a steep pull-up at 4,000ft, firing at 5,000ft at a high angle of attack to engage the flare towed behind the Jindivik drone flying at 14,000ft above. After cruising around the bay while range procedures are carried out, the FA 2 runs in accompanied by the chase aircraft for the 'hot' run. Weapons firing generally is very difficult to photograph, as the recording of the event must naturally take second place to the firing actually occurring, and it is only the flying of Lt 'Chips' Lawler that keeps us as a pair in the sharp pull up to witness the smokeless 9M come to life on the rail and streak off, completely soundless in the general noise of the T4(N). The missile travels at Mach 2 plus aircraft speed, successfully engaging the flare causing it to 'wobble', indicating passage within five feet of the target, with radio discipline temporarily disregarded after a good launch!

LEFT:
Evasion of such missiles is more difficult than public perception would believe, as they are unlikely to be launched by a competent pilot unless the chances of a kill are high. Hot burning rapid-bloom flares to decoy the seeker and chaff to confuse radars can be banged out, normally combined with a sharp change in direction and height. A programmable unit in the aircraft allows various loads, normally adjusted as operational conditions dictate and the perceived threat, with a combination of flares and chaff being a go/no go item in Bosnia. Here an FA 2 fires a selection of chaff, 218 (large) and 118 (small) flares.

BELOW:
For routine training a dummy acquisition missile and live head are fitted, to give realistic weights and drag but still allow practice engagements. The coolant to the head reduces 'clutter' in the infra-red detection ability in the head, and can be heard to have this effect on the ground during test. An immaculate FA 2 cuts through the upper air on simulated Combat Air Patrol with the drill head clearly visible.

OPPOSITE:
Rules of Engagement today dictate that to avoid 'blue on blue' friendly fire incidents the target should be positively visually identified (VID) prior to engagement. This drawback to the Fox 1 or head-on long-range missile means that unless a target is certainly hostile a close-in encounter may well ensue. This obviously requires the traditional skills of the dogfight, accurately described as 'a knife fight in a telephone box', so these skills are necessarily practised both in training and on the front line. In common with other fighter aircraft, the FA 2 has retained close-in weaponry after the failure of the American all-missile Phantoms in Vietnam, which proved both unreliable due to missile quality and inability to destroy at close range. Prior to Air Combat training the T4(N) tailchases the FA 2 at low-level and high G.

ABOVE:
The reliable and accurate 30mm Aden guns can be fitted in two pods either side of centreline, with magazines of 120 rounds per gun giving six seconds of fire at a cyclic rate of 1200 rpm. Saxe blue practice ammunition is used for strafing exercises ashore, but on board live HE rounds are used against the ship's splash target, which uses scoops to produce an easily visible water plume target at a safe distance from the ship. Called in on the circuit 'hot' by clansman radio, the squadron regularly practice this important skill, using cine film from the Pilot's Display Recorder camera to analyse results. This aircraft has returned from a shore range with a 'hang-up', where the pilot has attempted to fire the guns without success. The weapons supervisory team take over deck handling, pointing the aircraft outboard to minimise danger from misfire, while PO Dick Butcher and AEM Mark Pundyke clear the blockage – a spent cartridge – and leaf the ammunition back into the magazine.

Electrically fired by a wiper firing pin passing 115v AC across the base of the shell, the guns are fired out to sea in special range areas, using high explosive shells which explode on contact with the water to avoid danger from ricochets. The shell itself is only armed away from the aircraft, with a special fusing mechanism which is aligned by the centrifugal force imparted by the rifling spin. The spent cartridges and links can be seen dropping from ZD613 gunning off Lundy Island, with the noticeable lighter links blowing back in the airflow, occasionally causing tail strikes.

ABOVE:
The AMRAAM finally became front line operationally in July 1995, when live rounds that only arrived in the UK over the Easter period were finally fitted to the front line FA2s of 800 NAS. On the way to the Adriatic for another five-month period, squadron weapons' specialists practise loading-drills with a new missile.

LEFT:
The advent of the FA 2 finally brings the Sea Harrier and the Fleet Air Arm into the air superiority arena, giving the vital 'Fox 1' head-on long-range capability necessary for area defence at sea. Heavily loaded with four AMRAAM, two centreline and two outboard, the jet suffers little from the added load with only slight longitudinal instability. Previous missiles for the SHAR have all been 'clear air mass' weapons, requiring visual firing when in range, whereas AMRAAM can be fired IMC or in cloud giving true all-weather engagement possibilities. *(Phil Boyden BAe)*

ABOVE:
With this missile, targets can be engaged at a longer range than they can be detected with the FRS 1 Blue Fox, a quantum leap ahead. Described by pilots as 'a positive contribution to flight safety', ten missiles were fired in joint trials during 1993, conducting eject and rail test separations from the aircraft and the weapon performance against various targets. After 1.6 seconds the rocket motor pushes the missile off the rail, where it climbs at Mach 2.5 plus aircraft speed up to around 60,000ft, before acquiring the target and diving in at around 40/50 degrees. Mid-course guidance is passed via datalink with active terminal guidance, sophisticated anti-jam procedures meaning this is the missile you do not want to go head-to-head with.
(Elgin AFB USAF Official Photo)

RIGHT:
In the anti-shipping role, the Sea Harrier can carry two of the fearsome Sea Eagle missiles, fitted to the inboard pylons of this development aircraft during early trials over Brighton, East Sussex. This sea-skimming missile delivers a devastating punch to ship targets, tested in trials against old RN warships, resulting in the intentional sinking of the ex-HMS *Devonshire*. Delivery in formation at night is a testing sortie requiring excellent timing and planning, although the most dangerous task front line remains night surface attack with direct attack weapons such as bombs and rockets. *(Phil Boyden BAe)*

One of the major lessons learnt the hard way by the American forces in Vietnam was to practise air-to-air combat with different types, instead of one particular aircraft whose characteristics in combat are known as this can engender complacency. This rapidly became sound combat doctrine and today the Sea Harrier is no exception, conducting Dissimilar Act Combat Training (DACT) with other types both by detachment and hosting other air forces. The Spanish Matadors (effectively AV 8As) have several times flown to Yeovilton to take advantage of the high level of VSTOL combat experience at 899 NAS, being good for training as neither the FRS 1 or the Matador have BVR capabilities, therefore always closing to the dogfight. *(Phil Boyden BAe)*

Against head-on capable aircraft, tactics must of course be very different, demonstrated here in the form of the CF-18 Hornet of 439 Sqn RCAF. BVR capable aircraft rely on pulse-Doppler radars, which are countered by a great height split between the attacking pair of SHARs, attempting to lure the CF-18s to 'pass through' and open themselves up to a side or rear attack. Relying on the expertise of the fighter controller to pass target information or 'bogey dope' continuously, effectively using his radar as a second pair of eyes for the pilot, the air combat is always carefully briefed to include all relevant safety limitations, especially with very aggressive attacks such as head-to-head with guns, and is normally fought 'in the block' from the 5,000ft 'hard deck' up to 24,000ft.

OPPOSITE:
As previously discussed, airborne control of the Sea Harrier demands the cream of the Royal Navy's Observer aircrew. Launching well before the Sea Harriers take-off for Air Combat training to be within area, the Sea King AEW can take over Scene of Action command, vectoring assets against threats well before they are in range of the ship. An aircraft of 849 'A' flight returns from such a sortie, overflying a full deck park during an interesting period of FRS 1/FA 2 amalgamated operations, with the colour difference of the two types clearly visible.

The much vaunted and equally much misunderstood Vectoring In Forward Flight (VIFF) ability can also be used in various situations where rapid slow-down of the aircraft would give a tactical advantage. To VIFF the nozzles are pointed downwards to the hover position, and although the power of the engine is minor compared to the huge aerodynamic forces on the airframe, the SHAR will slow down quicker than a jet with constant rearward thrust. Useful in the vertical and in positions where height can rapidly be reconverted to airspeed by dropping the nose, this tactic when used correctly can cause a faster opponent to 'fly through' because he cannot decelerate at the same rate.

Descriptions of aerial combat seem rather analytical and do not give the impression of what is involved. Air combat is a sweaty, fast-moving and lethal pursuit, punctuated only by the laboured breathing of the pilots under high G, shouts, and the calm measured tones of the controller. The SHAR can pull up to 7G in combat, useful during rolling fights where the aircraft who pulls the most G can go 'nose-hot' first to engage. Under high humidity the manoeuvring aircraft produce contrails as the water vapour is forced from the air by the speed and G.

The more aircraft added to the equation, the more essential becomes pairs tactics and mutual cover. The FA 2 normally cruises on the opposite sides of an oval CAP station, with one aircraft remaining 'nose-hot' scanning the threat bearing. Identifying a possibly hostile contact, a technique called 'hook VID' is used to ID the contact whilst remaining in a strong position for engagement if necessary. The 'looker' flies straight towards the inbound threat VID on the way through, while the 'shooter' loops around to a covering position for immediate action. DACT is also carried out with RAF Hawks, which although without radar are high energy fighters, here outbound over the Gower Peninsula for three versus three air combat.

LEFT:
The SHAR is also an excellent bomber, with advanced and accurate software providing another capability used during the Falklands War on Port Stanley airfield. Up to five 1,000lb bombs can be carried, although fuel and recovery criteria mean that after launch four must be used or dropped safe. Regular use of shore range facilities giving a bombing 'footprint' of each individual aircraft software, analysed by the Air Warfare Instructor with PDR film showing a flag when the bomb is pickled off, giving optimum accuracy. The Carrier Bomb/Light Store (CBLS) is used for practice having the same aerodynamics as a real bomb, and can be filled with a variety of practice ordnance simulating various types.

BELOW:
The 14kg practice simulates a free-fall bomb profile, and the 3kg the retard bomb, the tail of which deploys a parachute to allow the aircraft time to escape prior to detonation at low-level. Lt Nick Weightmann flies an FA 2 fitted with guns and 3 CBLS during a close formation practice sortie with a T4(N).

RIGHT:
Weapon delivery varies according to the height of release, but invariably relies on visual acquisition followed by a roll and pull to stay visual in the dive. Should circumstances dictate, the bombs can also be dropped inert or 'safe' in the sea if not required. Loft bombing is also an option, allowing the weapon to adopt a ballistic trajectory to the target giving the aircraft time to escape on a reciprocal heading.

BELOW:
The ordnance is fitted to the aircraft by the Air Weapons specialisation in their characteristic red surcoats, known as 'bombheads' to the Fleet Air Arm, and its safe handling, fitting and use remains their responsibility until delivery. Using special hoists a practice bomb with a 114 ballistic tail is winched slowly into place, care being taken to locate the feet square in the release unit before the weapon is torque-loaded to the pylon, preventing any movement in flight.

ABOVE:
Operations over the former Yugoslavia with bombs need the capability to be deadly accurate, avoiding collateral damage as impressively demonstrated with Precision Guided Munitions during the Gulf War. The American laser-guided bombs were trialled by 800 NAS in 1993 after doubt about their use on the SHAR, as the aircraft has no equipment to actually detect the laser illumination cone projected upwards from the target. An interesting load for the weapon specialists due to the length of munition, it was assembled on deck and the guidance head and vanes tested for correct function before loading.

LEFT:
Final checks on the monster, clearly showing the two silver plugs containing the cartridges to blow the weapon off the SHAR. After launch the aircraft flew to a shore range where the bombs were successfully dropped using the accurate GPS satellite navigator, being unable to pick up the target designator. The bombs are an interesting sight to watch as they fall, 'bouncing' sharply off the sides of the invisible laser 'cone' at ever decreasing angles until impact onto the target with pinpoint accuracy.

75

The front line – otherwise known as the Sharp End – is the 'teeth' of the Royal Navy and the goal towards which all training effort is expended. A huge support infrastructure exists solely to ensure that ships can and do exercise regularly with their associated Naval aircraft, and personnel training is designed to ensure a constant flow of qualified and motivated people to sea. In the Fleet Air Arm fixed-wing world, most training is conducted by the headquarters of the Sea Harrier circuit, 899 NAS at Royal Naval Air Station Yeovilton in Somerset. Both aircrew and maintainers train here, rotating as drafted to the front line but invariably returning to 899 for refresher training, advancement and second line service at the shore base. The squadron itself has a long and illustrious history, with many battle honours testifying to the wide variety of conflicts supported, and also has the traditional role of a pool of experience and aircraft which can be drawn upon in emergency.

899 NAS – motto 'Strike and Defend' – was formed at Hatston in December 1942 with the Seafire 11C derivative of the Spitfire fighter. Embarked in HMS *Indomitable* in July 1943, the squadron provided fighter cover for the Sicily landings, duplicating this role from HMS *Hunter* for the Salerno operations. Armed with the later variant of the Seafire, the L111, shore and shipping were attacked in the Crete area whilst on board HMS *Khendive*. Deck training for the newly-formed Australian Fleet Air Arm followed, until at the end of hostilities the squadron was disbanded. Re-formed in 1955 with Sea Hawk aircraft, the squadron's tradition of supporting the front line was upheld when the squadron personnel deployed on board HMS *Eagle* in April 1956, assisted in the comprehensive emasculation of the Egyptian Air Force as their contribution to the Suez Affair. Again disbanded after action, the squadron was resurrected as the Sea Vixen FAW 1 HQ squadron, remaining mainly shore-based but detaching as required to sea. When the Sea Vixen returned as the FAW 2, the unit formed the nucleus of the Intensive Flying Trials Unit, testing the aircraft in home and Mediterranean waters before disbandment.

On 31 March 1980 the squadron re-formed from the elements of the 700A Flt Sea Harrier IFTU at RNAS Yeovilton. Weapon validation trials and training occupied the months before the Falklands conflict, when once again the aircraft and personnel embarked and fought from the two carriers. Returning successfully, the squadron has continued to convert pilots to the SHAR using the two-seat T4(N) train maintainers for the two front line units and most recently, to establish the Operational Evaluation Unit for the newly-introduced FA 2. Celebrating the 50th Anniversary of the formation of the unit, in 1992 the whole squadron demonstrated 100 per cent serviceability for a flypast including the Flag Officer Naval Aviation, Rear-Admiral Colin Cooke-Priest RN.

Small deployments of the new jet to aircraft carriers have been undertaken, as well as regular deployments to air combat ranges in the North Sea and Decimommanu in Sardinia. Other units regularly visit, recognising the value of Dissimilar Air Combat training with the unique Sea Harrier, and the squadron is now optimistic in looking forward to its longest period in commission as the Sea Harrier looks likely to serve the Fleet Air Arm well into the 21st Century.

The two front line squadrons have an equally distinguished history, formed on the same date of 3 April 1933, and possess much of the friendly rivalry often associated with closely linked units. 800 NAS – motto *Nunquam Non Paratus* (Never unprepared) – was the first jet unit in the FAA, formed as a fleet fighter squadron with Nimrod and Osprey biplane aircraft initially flying from HMS *Courageous* in home and Mediterranean waters. Joining HMS *Ark Royal* with the Skua, the German capital ship *Konigsberg* was bombed as she lay in Bergen harbour during the invasion of Norway. During this same campaign six He 111 bombers were shot down, although four aircraft were lost during a punishing attempt to attack the *Scharnhorst*. Further action followed as fighter cover for the fleet during the sinking of the French fleet at Oran, following which the squadron refitted with Sea Hurricanes to support the North African landings.

Continuously in action and frequently changing aircraft types as war provided the spur, Hellcats of the unit took part in attacks on the *Tirpitz* before her final appointment with 617 Squadron RAF. Post war, the unit operated the Seafire in Malaysia, followed by the Sea Hawk FGA 6 from HMS *Albion* during the Suez crisis, progressing through the Scimitar and Buccaneer to eventual disbandment in February 1972. Re-formed on 31 March 1980 with four Sea Harrier FRS 1s, the unit played a major part during the Falklands War on board HMS *Hermes*, and has since been rotated as required to all three aircraft carriers.

801 NAS – motto *On les aura* (We'll get them) – formed at Netheravon, also as a fleet fighter squadron but armed with Flycatchers and Nimrods. Service with HMS *Furious* and refitting with Sea Gladiators was followed by amalgamation with other units, as control of the Fleet Air Arm was wrestled from the RAF. Sea Hurricanes armed the squadron when re-formed in 1941, embarking to HMS *Eagle* to protect the Malta convoys. After seeing a small amount of action the ship was torpedoed and sunk on 11 August, with the bulk of the aircraft being lost – those airborne at the time being absorbed into other units. Now with Seafires in HMS *Furious*, 801 supported the North Africa landings with 800 and also flew top cover for the *Tirpitz* raids in 1944. Service in the Far East followed, including participation in the decimation of the Japanese fleet at Truk lagoon in the Philippines, known as the American revenge for Pearl Harbor. In common with many hostilities-only squadrons, disbandment on return to the UK followed. Re-formed again post war, in swift succession the Sea Fury followed the Sea Hornet, until the arrival of the first jet in the shape of the Sea Hawk FGA 6. After assisting the RAF in Aden operations in July 1958, this type was superseded by the Buccaneer S2, flown from HMS *Victorious* and *Hermes* until disbandment in 1970. Re-formed again on 28 January 1981 with five Sea Harrier FRS 1 aircraft, this unit too demonstrated their professionalism in the Falklands from HMS *Invincible*. They too are now deployed as required on the allocated aircraft carrier for front line service.

Each front line squadron is made up of approximately ten aircrew, three Air Engineering Officers and one hundred and ten ratings, forming an independent self-contained unit to operate six or seven Sea Harriers. The Commanding Officer, normally a senior officer of Lieutenant-Commander rank, remains responsible to the command for the conduct and operational readiness of his unit, with his authority being delegated where required within the squadron to achieve the task. The Senior Pilot, normally of similar rank to the CO, co-ordinates flying activities and to him falls much of the day-to-day running of the squadron, from organising

training packages to more general Naval duties. Additionally other experienced aircrew officers will fill the posts of Qualified Flying Instructor (QFI) and Air Warfare Instructor (AWI), responsible for continuation training and maintenance of standards. Ratings are administered through the Naval Divisional system through Senior Rates to Junior Ratings of different departments, with a nominated officer charged with the welfare of up to ten ratings via this chain. The Regulating Chief Petty Officer remains responsible for discipline and general personnel administration in consultation with upper management, and is generally viewed as the man who runs the squadron day-to-day. Normally split into three watches working eight hours about, the maintainers also come under the authority of the Air Engineering Officers through the chain of command. This seemingly rigid chain of delegation actually allows a great deal of flexibility, enabling rapid changes to be implemented as they occur and allowing the squadron to bond together as a unit with great team spirit.

Based at RNAS Yeovilton in Somerset, the squadrons work hard when ashore, training the small but continuous number of recently-qualified aircrew coming through the pipeline and maintaining more senior pilots currency in the air, including night qualification which must be validated from an airfield before practised on a ship. Long into the night over rural Somerset the Sea Harriers can be heard, out and inbound from practice sorties going to one of the hover pads at the air station for night recoveries. Regular detachments are made for weapons camps, exercises with other airforces and of course to the aircraft carriers when at sea, and although they always return to Yeovilton, the squadrons spend a considerable amount of their time away from home. Embarkation to the ships involves a huge logistic exercise, transporting personnel, spares and records to Portsmouth in time to sail, as the aircraft themselves are invariably embarked at sea south of the Isle of Wight or in the South-West Approaches.

The hard work whilst disembarked is needed to bring the squadron up to pre-embarkation readiness, as immediately upon embarkation, flying operations commence to bring the unit to operational readiness within a given period of time. Short but intense work-up periods normally precede long-term deployment, highlighting weak areas to inspection teams who indicate required remedial actions in no uncertain terms. Once the squadron is up to operational standards the task can be met as dictated by the command, and the Sea Harrier and its dedicated air and groundcrew will once again be ready to perform any task that is allocated to them and to perform it in the best traditions of the Fleet Air Arm.

Sea Harrier tasking from the ship follows the designation of the FRS 1, namely organic air support for the Fleet, reconnaissance and strike on both land and sea. Combat Air Patrol (CAP) and Airborne Intercepts controlled both by the carrier and 'bags' (AEW Sea Kings), are regularly exercised by day and night to cement the ability to intercept and destroy targets inbound for the ship, and obviously this capability alone has been much enhanced by the introduction of the FA 2 and its area-denial all-weather radar and missile combination. With the notable exception of Battle Damage Assessment in the Falklands, reconnaissance remained really little more than an under-utilised extra on the aircraft, until the 'Deny Flight' operations over Bosnia-Hertzegovena in 1993-5 showed that once again the aircraft could also deliver this role. Strike, however, always remained firmly in practice, both with the Sea Eagle sea-skimming missile and bombs. Whilst tactical doctrines remain classified, four-ship formations regularly practise missile launch simulation tactics at night, with the devastating punch of the Sea Eagle being tested several times in the 1980s on old Royal Navy warships. Weapons detachments to ranges that permit live bombing and gunning are arranged, with weapon delivery and analysis being supervised by the squadron Air Warfare Instructor. Tactics and enhanced software in the FA 2 promise an enhancement of these traditional aircraft roles into the Twenty-First Century, reflected in the designation Fighter Attack.

OVERLEAF:
The flight-deck of an aircraft carrier is rightly considered to be one of the most dangerous places in the world. High noise levels, rotor discs, jet intakes and blast combine to make the deck an interesting environment, and one that can only be rendered safe by good leadership, communication and practices. Awaiting the order to taxi from the deck park aft under control of the aircraft handler, the chain lashings on the nosewheel hold the aircraft secure as the ship turns onto the Designated Flying Course (DFC).

ABOVE:
In hot and humid climates the engine performance is degraded, requiring water injection to the engine for maximum thrust on take-off. The water flow is tested in the No-Go VTO where nozzles are checked fully down by the Air Engineering Officer (AEO) before the pilot applies full power to check water flow. After obtaining the green cockpit light indication and 108% thrust (as opposed to 104% 'dry'), the throttle is closed back to idle and the aircraft taxied forward to the allocated deck position, under the direction of the Flight Deck Officer (FDO) or his opposite watch deputy the Chief of the Flight Deck (CFD). No-go VTO checks occasionally produce a red beam of power from the hot aft nozzles at 650 degrees centigrade, seen here as the 800 NAS aircraft creates two red hot spots on the deck.

ABOVE:
The FDO does final checks on the aircraft, keeping safety paramount by checking the Master Armament Safety Switch (MASS) is live (in case the pilot needs to 'bang off' the tanks for emergency weight reasons) and he can see two ejection seat pins. A green traffic-style light under Flyco gives command approval, and the FDO's green flag is held up to signify final launch permission to the pilot. Brakes on, full power selected, nozzles 10 degrees down to avoid damaging the tailplane, and brakes off at 55% power, the SHAR thunders off down the deck within fifteen feet of the FDO stood on the wingtip safety line.

LEFT:
Halfway down the deck the aircraft has reached 50 knots as the hot blast hits the CFD and AEO, subjecting them to winds in excess of seventy knots plus ship's speed. Goggles are necessary to prevent eye damage as the grit in the Camrex deck covering is blown free, giving a 'shot blast' effect combining with the water blasted from the ringbolt wells.

RIGHT:
Once airborne, a variety of sorties are undertaken including Airborne Intercepts under control of the 'bags' of 849 NAS, exercising the Fighter Controllers and close-in weapons crews. The fuel-critical SHAR gives around an hour on task before the 'hard charlie' recovery time approaches, requiring return to the ship under control of 'Homer', the call-sign of the ship's Air Traffic Controllers.

BELOW:
The enhanced ramp angle of 12 degrees has the double advantage of imparting a ballistic trajectory to the aircraft away from the sea whatever ship movement, and giving an extra 2,000lb payload for the same length take-off run. As the white line on the end of the ramp passes through the periphery of the pilot's vision, he selects 35 degrees nozzle down to arrest the sink rate once airborne before trimming them aft again slowly to pick up airspeed away from the ship, climbing nose-high at 12 units angle of attack with gear retracted at 220 knots.

Coming under control of 'Homer' at 30 miles the pair report in at 15 nautical miles from the carrier, forming a 'cakestand' stack 1,000ft apart until individually called in for either Carrier Controlled or Pilot Initiated Approach as weather dictates.

ABOVE:
The high cyclic rate of SHAR operations reflects not only good aircraft serviceability but a highly intensive work period from the squadron. Regularly turning in serviceability rates of 90% plus, during 1993-4 800 NAS did not miss a single tasked recce sortie in Bosnia – a record favourably commented upon by the United Nations.

RIGHT:
Early problems resulting in undemanded movements of the flight-deck lifts, in one case dumping a Sea King AEW upright in the lift well, have now been solved with the platforms proving reliable and safe. During 18 months HMS *Ark Royal*'s lifts cycled over 18,000 times without incident, raised and lowered by hydraulic rams connected to the platforms by giant 'Y' struts. At the end of the flying day the SHARs requiring deep maintenance are dropped down the forward lift into the hangar, where constant round the clock servicing is carried out by squadron personnel on an eight-hour watch system.

The forward hangar is optimised for SHAR maintenance at sea, with a good air stores system allowing major engineering jobs such as engine changing, where the whole wing is removed by crane to allow access. Working the equivalent of an 84-hour week, the maintainers are capable of deep engineering work, assisted by the excellent stores system biased towards keeping the front line operational.

Final checks complete, the ground crew hold up all the locks and pins from the aircraft for visual inspection. The pilot nods to the 'plane captain', the maintenance rating allocated to each particular aircraft, and the SHAR is now ready to taxi into position for the no-go VTO prior to take-off.

ABOVE:
Once airborne the aircraft join into a pair in close formation as they transit through cloud up to the sun above. Reference points are selected on the leader, such as inboard pylon in line with front cold nozzle, and the pilot endeavours to keep these in line during the climb. Close formation for SHAR pilots is very close indeed, best appreciated from the back seat of a T4(N) recovering through cloud.

LEFT:
FlyCo controls the visual circuit around the carrier, deck movements and general flight safety in the deck environment. Commander (AIR) is the ultimate authority on aviation matters, responsible for the conduct of all flying operations to the Command, and is normally a senior aircrew officer with decades of experience. Head of the Air Department, he has deputies through which his authority is delegated, seen here in FlyCo supervising SHAR recoveries as an aircraft comes across one spot.

RIGHT:
The more unpleasant characteristics of unpowered or uncontrolled VSTOL flight were investigated by Martin-Baker when considering escape systems for the Harrier. Vertical sink rates of up to 80 feet per second were encountered during trials, requiring an extremely powerful seat with a large rocket pack. The Mk 10 pooled all the company's experience and knowledge into a single design originally meant for the Tornado, putting the pilot on a fully deployed parachute in 2.95 seconds. The rapid deployment GQ aeroconical parachute contributes immensely to the success of this seat, which has saved seventeen Sea Harrier aircrew in the same number of ejections.

OPPOSITE:
The after-deck park holds eight aircraft at a push, mainwheels of each aircraft moved to within one inch of the lip that surrounds the deck. This puts fifteen feet of jet tail directly over the sea, causing problems in inserting the catwalk-mounted telebriefing cables in their tail sockets.

ABOVE:
A comprehensive walkround inspection of the aircraft is undertaken by the pilot, accompanied by the plane captain as he ensures the jet is not damaged in any way and fully serviceable for the sortie. The vent doors on the intakes can occasionally jam after an engine pop surge, and are checked here by Lt-Cdr David Baddams prior to duskers night flying in the French exercise areas off Toulon.

OVERLEAF:
Wet deck operations are particularly demanding for the ground crews, being subjected to the blast repeatedly throughout launches. A spectacular sight from higher decks, this picture shows the conditions experienced at flight-deck level as the CFD CPO Nick Wilkin is hit by the blast from the jet, obliterating visibility instantly into white-out conditions – not good for cameras!

LEFT:
Calculated on the power of the best engine, established on check test flights, the length of the flight deck run is calculated to have the aircraft at exactly 90 knots when it hits the slight lip at the base of the ramp, avoiding nose oleo compression if going too fast yet attaining maximum ballistic energy for take-off. The FDO is seen here chalking the two sets of figures passed to him for take-offs by both the FRS 1 and the slightly heavier FA 2 during the Adriatic trial period. Chalk cannot be removed by blast and can be read at day and night, and in this position is unlikely to be mislaid.

BELOW:
'Deny Flight' operations require tanking before entering Bosnia via certain ATC 'gate' points near Split, as the airspace is heavily policed by American, French and RAF fighters in addition to the Royal Navy. An oval tanking line is established over the small islands on the west coast, where the tanker refuels one of the pair over the island of Otoc Vis on 13 September 1993.

Approach to the Tristar is faster and conducted under tactical restraints, with a high rate fuel flow giving full tanks within five or six minutes. This astonishing wide-angle shot shows the view from XZ494 plugged into the Tristar at 276 knots and 10,600 feet.

High over the mountainous terrain south east of Donji Ribnik in Bosnia Hertzegovena, the number two of the pair breaks to starboard displaying the 9M sidewinders and belly-mounted Aden guns. The aircraft have just finished a Close Air Support mission under the control of a French Forward Air Controller on a bunker HQ building at Cazin north-west of Bihac, practising the normal bombing procedure and staying above the 5000ft ceiling imposed to avoid small-arms fire from the trigger-happy combatants below.

After a final busy and successful period on station in the Adriatic, the Sea Harrier FRS 1s of 800 NAS received three days deep maintenance prior to flying off to RNAS Yeovilton for the last time. Fittingly the Commanding Officer's aircraft (122/XZ494) was marked with the dates of service of the type, and he led the squadron as they disembarked from the *Invincible* on Saturday, 25 February 1995, formating to fly past once in salute below the grey clouds before climbing away, never to return.

BELOW:
Weather in the Adriatic is not always as clear and bright as can be imagined. Two SHAR return from another CAS/CAP mission at midday in rain showers, closer together than normal due to the poor visibility. Recovery starts at ten nautical miles with checks for landing, proceeding to the four mile point where the ship passes range and advisory height to the jets, establishing a three degree glide-path. Decelerating around 400 yards short of the ship's stern, a hover is established as the Landing Safety Officer (normally squadron duty officer) watches and advises from FlyCo while the pair recover safely.

Returning to RNAS Yeovilton in late
February 1995 from 800 NAS, the last FRS
1s will be quickly replaced by the FA 2
and converted in turn to this standard.
Serving front line for fifteen years, combat
proven and a vindication of VSTOL air
power at sea, the success of the Sea Harrier
can be attributed to an excellent basic
design and the hard work of the Royal
Navy to make it a success. In this
atmospheric shot in typical Somerset
weather, large clouds provide an
impressive backdrop to the two aircraft
flying over the A303 whilst orbiting the
field on long finals.

OVERLEAF:
A deckful of FA 2s on board HMS
Invincible for the first time, as the CO of
899 NAS climbs out after embarking to the
ship in August 1994. The FA 2 is not
supersonic capable, whereas the FRS 1
could be dived through the speed of sound
without tanks, regarded by those in the
know as 'not a sane thing to do'.

ABOVE:
The FA 2 tactics currently under development require the pair to establish a CAP station 30 miles from the ship, up threat with a Sea King AEW off to the side providing an additional picture to complement the 996 radar onboard. The fighter controller and the AEW observer liaise to control and vector the fighters, the agency with the best picture assuming control as propagation may degrade one of the radars. The Sea Harriers assume an oval orbit, keeping one aircraft 'nose-hot' up the threat bearing at all times.

LEFT:
Only 500lb heavier than the FRS 1, the FA 2 comes across the deck using around 99% of the 104% power available in 'dry' conditions. After transition across the deck, power is reduced momentarily to assess sink rate and reapplied to cushion the landing, with late application of power producing the power bounce effect sometimes observed.

ABOVE:
Two FA 2 aircraft have been lost in unrelated incidents, both by a bizarre coincidence sharing the side number 713. Understandably the OEU decided that no further airframes would bear this traditionally bad-luck side number, so a compromise was reached to sequentially number the 'cabs' 712, 712½ and 714. 712½ is seen here during pre-deployment training off Portland taking part in the weekly 'Thursday War' serial, exercising the ship at action stations.

RIGHT:
The white line running up the deck on the right-hand side of the runway is known as the 'wingtip safety line', inside which no-one is permitted during launch for health reasons. Seconds before the launch, under supervision the wingtip safety line is crossed and this unique head-on view of two jets on the runway is obtained.

LEFT:
Aircraft carriers possess a fully-fitted photographic section, manned with Navy-trained professional photographers to support the reconnaissance efforts of the squadron, provide defect/crash cover and occasionally taking public relations pictures for the ship. Access to areas not normally permitted can be obtained with some pressure, allowing some interesting positions to be attained for photography, demonstrated here as the author covers the launch of an FA 2 from the goalkeeper platform on the ship's bows.

BELOW:
Practised at Yeovilton on the dummy deck prior to the front line, the overriding impression of ramp launch to the passenger is the extremely short take-off and noticeable ballistic trajectory, like literally being 'thrown' off the ski jump. An FA 2 is seen the instant it clears the ramp with full flap and the nozzles travelling to 35 degrees, arresting the sink rate as the ballistic trajectory decreases and the airspeed increases.

Superb cockpit imagery obtained over
Bosnia using the 16mm lens on the Nikon
F90, showing the pilot's-eye view holding
station with the tanker during refuelling
on the normal tanker line. The accurate
GPS navigator sits on the left-hand side of
the cockpit arch, with the ejection seat
pins also clearly visible in their stowage
on the right.

LEFT:
The other aircraft of the pair hangs off the tanker in contact over the small islands of Otok Korcula off the Yugoslav coast, prior to heading inland for CAS exercising with a Malaysian Forward Air Controller.

BELOW:
The FAC uses large ground features, such as Split International Airport underneath this FA 2, to initially bring the eyes of a pilot into a rough area before utilising smaller features such as roads and rivers pinpointing the target location. NATO common codewords, mainly of American origin, allow FACs of many different nations to co-ordinate operations visually, although language and pronunciation difficulties can cause some unintentional humour.

Call-sign 'Magic', on station an AWACS
Boeing 707 acts as control authority,
overseeing a vast tract of airspace over the
region and vectoring the Sea Harriers onto
contacts of interest as they arise, with the
ship also staying in communication using
Havequick frequency agile radios.
Returning from simulated CAP over
Somerset, two FA 2s descend through the
lower air towards Yeovilton.

RIGHT:
Another sortie over, the pair rejoin for low
finals past the goalkeeper weapons system
on the forecastle of the ship. The FA 2 is
likely to remain in service well into the
next century, with modification becoming
an excellent area denial and defence
fighter.

APPENDIX
SEA HARRIER AIRFRAME LISTINGS

By Brian Johnstone MBE

Brian Johnstone has served in the fixed-wing Fleet Air Arm since 1967, working on the Sea Vixen and Phantom before the introduction of the Sea Harrier. Having joined 800 NAS two weeks before the official commissioning date in March 1980, Brian served on board HMS *Hermes* during the Falklands conflict and has since completed several front line tours of duty, with his years of service being recognised with the award of the MBE. Throughout this time he has maintained his own airframe records, and now holds the most comprehensive details available anywhere, with information obtained at first-hand from aircraft log books, combat data sheets and squadron fair flying logs. I am most grateful to him for providing this information, allowing the production of the most accurate list ever published.

Abbreviations: A/F hours – Airframe hours : F/F – First Flight : D/D – Delivery date : W/O – Written-off.

XZ438 F/F – 30.12.78. BAe and A & AEE development aircraft. *Hermes* 13–23.7.81 for ramp trials; disembarked following engine overtemp. D/D to VL 19.4.82 for 809 NAS use painted in light grey colour scheme. Used for various ramp trials until W/O 17.5.82 due to fuel transfer/imbalance problem whilst taking-off from ramp with 330-gallon ferry tanks. Pilot Lt-Cdr D. Poole ejected safely suffering minor injuries. A/F hours at W/O 224.50.

XZ439 F/F – 30.3.79 (Pilot M. Snelling). BAe and A & AEE development aircraft. *Hermes* 24.10.79–8.11.79 deck trials. *Invincible* Oct '80 for deck trials; first aircraft to ramp launch at sea 30.10.80 (Pilot M. Snelling). D/D to VL at A/F 304.00 hrs for 809 NAS use and painted in light grey colour scheme. Loaned to BAe returning to 899 NAS for Farnborough display 4–13.9.82 flown by Lt-Cdr Thomas. D/D 27.9.82 to BAe for resumption of trials programme and flown at Paris Air Show May '83 in 899 markings with code 19. Converted to FA 2 by October '89 continues as trials aircraft to date.

XZ440 F/F – 6.6.79 (Pilot M. Snelling). BAe and A & AEE development aircraft. *Hermes* 24.10–8.11.79 deck trials. *Invincible* Oct '80

second ramp launch at sea. D/D 3.6.82 for 899 returned to BAe custody 25.6.82. Used for trials of 190-gallon drop tanks and twin Sidewinder installation prior to 809 NAS deployment to *Illustrious* South Atlantic 1982. Sea Eagle development aircraft. At VL 17–18.2.84 for ramp trials with Sea Eagle and again 29.2.89 with Sea Eagle and Sidewinders. D/D 2.4.86 to St Athan for Phase 1 update and conversion to service (removal of trials equipment and wiring). D/D 27.5.88 to 800 recoded 126. Loaned to 801 28.3.89 returning to 800 22.4.89. 29.10.89 on *Invincible* aircraft suffered CAT 4 damage when fuel system was over-pressurised; returning to UK from US in RAF C-130. 6.7.90 to BAe for repair and conversion to FA 2.

XZ450 F/F – 20.8.78 (Pilot J. Farley – maiden flight). BAe and A & AEE development aircraft. First public appearance Farnborough 3.9.78 coded M on fin. First embarkation *Hermes* 13–18.11.78 flew 10 sorties. Nav kit trials RFA Olwen 7–10.4.79 recorded 50 on fin. Aircraft operated daily from Dunsfold but stayed overnight on board 9/10. Paris Air Show 9–17.6.79. D/D 3.4.82 to 800 NAS at VL 4.4.82 landing on *Hermes* alongside Portsmouth dockyard. 1

May attacked Port Stanley airfield Flt Lt Ball dropping three 1,000lb bombs. Next sortie 4 May, aircraft shot down over Goose Green with loss of pilot Lt N Taylor RN. It is possible that the loss of this aircraft may have helped keep the Argentinian Navy in harbour, as it was used for Sea Eagle trials. Examination of the wreckage may have given the impression that all Sea Harriers were Sea Eagle capable, a considerable threat to their ships.

XZ451 F/F – 25.5.79 (Pilot H. Frick). First aircraft for the RN D/D 18.6.79 at 3.08 A/F hrs to 700A coded 100. *Hermes* 24.10–8.11.79 for trials. First RN public appearance Culdrose 25.7.79. D/D 31.3.80 to 899 coded 100 recoded 710 7.81. At St Athan 10–28.4.81 for radio mods. D/D 4.4.82 to 801 coded 006. 1.5.82 Lt-Cdr 'Sharkey' Ward damaged an Argentinian Mentor with cannon fire, with the same aircraft flown by Lt Curtis in the evening downing a Canberra with Sidewinders. 21.5.82 Lt-Cdr 'Sharkey' Ward shot down a Pucara with cannon and a Hercules C-130 with Sidewinder and cannon. Three confirmed kills – 1 Canberra, 1 Pucara and 1 C-130. D/D 17.9.82 to 800 returned to 801 18.10.82 – recoded 008 15.12.82 and 000 on 10.1.83. Resprayed at

Dunsfold '84, D/D 11.12.86 to 899 NAS coded 712. 10.7.87 to St Athan for Phase 1 update. D/D 22.1.88 to 801 coded 003 then to 800 24.3.88 coded 123. 24.5.88 to AMG then by road to St Athan 23.6.88 returning to AMG 13.1.89. D/D 31.1.89 to 801 coded 005. W/O near Sardinia 1.12.89 following control restriction; Pilot Lt M. Auckland RN ejected safely.

XZ452 F/F – 17.8.79. (Pilot M. Snelling). D/D 12.10.79 to 700A coded 101. *Hermes* trials 24.10–8.11.79. CAT 3 damage to rear fuel tank around 5.3.80 transferred to SU for repair. Test-flown prior to D/D 16.3.81 to St Athan for respray. D/D 4.4.81 to 899 NAS coded 101 recoded 711 7.81. D/D 4.4.82 to 801 recoded 007. On 1.5.82 Flt Lt Barton shot down an Argentinian Mirage III with Sidewinder. Confirmed kill 1 Mirage. W/O 6.5.82 Lt-Cdr Eyton-Jones killed investigating surface contact with XZ453. Both aircraft either collided or flew into the sea in bad weather.

XZ453 F/F – 5.12.79. (Pilot J. Farley). D/D 31.1.80 to 700A coded 105. D/D 31.3.80 to 899 recoded 715 by 7.81. D/D 4.4.82 to 801 recoded 009. On 1.5.82 pilot Lt Thomas engaged a Mirage III with Sidewinder, with the Mirage sufficiently damaged to attempt to land at Port Stanley airfield, subsequently shot down by Argentinian defenders. 1 shared kill – Mirage. W/O 6.5.82, pilot Lt Curtis killed with ZX452 (as above).

XZ454 F/F – 12.12.79. (Pilot H. Frick). D/D 15.2.80 to 800 coded 250 officially to 800 31.3.80. First Sea Harrier to land on *Invincible* 20.5.80. W/O 1.12.80 at 235.35 A/F hours Lt-Cdr M. Blissett struck top of *Invincible* ramp during flypast, pilot ejected sustaining eye injuries.

XZ455 F/F – 9.10.79. (Pilot H. Frick). D/D 9.10.79 at 2.20 A/F hours to 700A coded 102. D/D 5.4.82 to 800 joining *Hermes* in English Channel after sailing from Portsmouth coded 12. On 1.5.82 Flt Lt Penfold dropped three 1,000lb bombs and expended 200 30mm rounds on Port Stanley airfield, shooting down an Argentinian Dagger aircraft later same day with Sidewinder missile. 21.5.82 Lt-Cdr R. Frederiksen shot down another Dagger with Sidewinder. Between 1.5.–14.6 aircraft flew 58 sorties dropping 28 1,000lb bombs, firing 200 rounds of 30mm cannon and firing two Sidewinders. Two confirmed kills – Argentinian

Daggers. Typical bombing sorties during this time include; 12.5.82 Lt Hargreaves Stanley airfield 1,000lb bomb, 29.5.82 Lt McHarg Pebble Island three 1,000lb bombs. 4.7.82 transferred to 801 NAS recoded 000. D/D 17.9.82 to 899 coded 715. D/D 14.9.83 to 800 coded 127. Resprayed at Dunsfold June. 19.2.87 aircraft severely damaged at RAF Linton-on-Ouse when both drop tanks ripped off damaging wing and tailplane. To AIU Lee 4.3.87 by road and on to St Athan 14.8.87 for phase 1 update (fuselage only). D/D 25.4.88 to 899 coded 712. AMG then D/D 8.6.90 to 899 NAS coded 715. D/D 20.2.92 to St Athan then conversion to FA 2 at Dunsfold. D/D 2.2.94 to 899 coded 717 and 6.10.94 to 801 coded 001.

XZ456 F/F – 9.11.79 (Pilot H. Frick). D/D 4.1.80 to 700A coded 103 then to 899 as 103 31.3.80. D/D 4.4.82 to 801 recoded 008. Flown by Lt-Cdr T. Gedge 23.5.82 shares destruction of grounded Puma and expended nine 1,000lb bombs. W/O 1.6.82 brought down by Roland AAM, pilot Flt Lt Ian Mortimer ejected safely landing in the sea off Port Stanley.

XZ457 F/F – 15.12.79 (Pilot J. Farley). D/D 31.1.80 at 2:13 A/F to 700A coded 104. Loaned to BAe for Farnborough display 1–7.9.80. D/D 2.4.82 to 800 recoded 14. 1.5.82 Lt McHarg bombed Darwin airstrip (Goose Green) with three 1,000lb bombs and expends 200 rounds 30mm. 2.5.82 two sorties using a further 280 rounds 30mm. 21.5.82 Lt Morell engaged two A4Q Skyhawks with Sidewinder, destroying one but second missile misfired. Target then badly damaged with 30mm, attempting to land at Stanley until pilot ejected due to severe oleo damage. 24.5.82 Lt-Cdr Auld intercepts flight of Daggers, again engaging with Sidewinder destroying two aircraft. Final record four confirmed kills – 2 A4Q Skyhawks and two Daggers, with three 1,000lb bombs dropped and 680 rounds 30mm fired on 66 operational sorties. D/D 19.7.82 to 899 recoded 713 after appearing at Farnborough 4–13.9.82. Phase one update 11.9.87 then to 800 18.3.88. AMG 25.9.89 then D/D 6.4.90 to 801 coded 003. 6.1.92 to 899 prior to FA 2 conversion at Dunsfold. D/D 10.3.94 to 899 FA2 coded 714 to date.

XZ458 F/F – 10.1.80 (Pilot H. Frick). D/D 22.2.80 at 3:50 A/F hrs to 800 coded 251. First embarked engine change *Invincible* Oct 80 recoded

124. D/D 7.4.82 to 899 and 809 15.5. repainted in 809 medium grey scheme and flown south 30.4 to Banjul, Gambia in 6 hr ferry flight. Embarked *Atlantic Conveyor* 6.5.82 transferring to 801 19.5.82 coded 007 – flew 45 operational sorties in area. To Yeovilton 6.12.82 then St Athan. D/D 11.4.84 to 800 coded 125. W/O 1.12.84 at 1285:45 A/F hrs near Fort William, Scotland due to birdstrike initiated engine failure – pilot Lt Collier suffered eye injuries.

XZ459 F/F – 21.3.80 (Pilot H. Frick). D/D 15.5.80 at 3:58 AF hrs to 800 NAS coded 252. Radio mods at St Athan then recoded 25 en route to Falklands 4.82. 1.5.82 dropped three 1,000lb bombs on Stanley runway pilot Lt-Cdr Batt. Flew 53 sorties in area, dropping nine 1,000lb bombs and firing 200 rounds 30mm. No significant kills but took part in destruction of freighter *Rio Carcarana* flown by Lt-Cdr Batt. D/D 22.7.82 to 809 coded 256 and on return from South Atlantic to 899 6.12.82 coded 716. D/D 20.9.84 to 801 coded 001. Then Phase 1 update 4.11.86. D/D 4.6.87 to 899 coded 717. 12.10.93 to St Athan then Dunsfold for conversion to FA 2.

XZ460 F/F – 10.4.80 (Pilot T. Scott). D/D 29.5.80 to 800 coded 253 at 3:06 A/F hrs. To Falklands recoded as 26, dropped cluster bombs on Darwin airstrip 1.5.82. 9.5.82 expended 200 rounds 30mm and one 1,000lb bomb, used by Lt-Cdr Batt to disable the spy trawler *Narwal*. 22.5.82 Lt-Cdr Frederiksen strafed patrol ship *Rio Iguaza*, causing it to beach. Final total – share in damaging two vessels, dropped 16 1,000lb bombs and fired 400 rounds of 30mm. D/D 19.7.82 to 899 coded 710. 29.8.88 899 coded 719 then 800 1.90 coded 128. W/O 9.5.90 flown into sea just after take-off from *Invincible* – pilot Lt Holmes killed.

XZ491 F/F – 20.6.80 (Pilot H. Frick). Initial service with BAe and A&AEE. 14.4.82 to 809 flown south to Banjul, Gambia in 6 hours by Lt Covington joining *Atlantic Conveyor* at Ascension. Flew 47 sorties in theatre without incident. D/D 6.12.82 to 801 recoded 002 then 2.2.83 to 899 recoded 711. To 801 as 000 by late 85, W/O 16.4.86 when aircraft ran out of fuel – pilot Lt-Cdr Sinclair ejected safely.

XZ492 F/F – 25.10.80 (Pilot J. Farley). D/D 29.12.80 at 2:59 A/F hours to 800 coded 254. Landing accident 15.5.81 RAF Leuchars when

At 900ft AGL, ZD607/127 leads 800 NAS orbiting overhead Stourhead Gardens in Somerset before running in to display at RNAS Yeovilton. High humidity gives the cloud effect over the wings as the formation pulls 3G to stay tight on the leader.

Raw Power – the fine lines of the SHAR
fighter flown by Lt-Cdr Don Sigourney,
shown to advantage in this view dumping
fuel into the sunset pulling high G.

outrigger torn off on runway barrier. 1.5.82 Lt Morell drops three 1,000lb bombs on Stanley, and 21.5.82 Lt Thomas shoots down Skyhawk with AIM 9L. Final totals ZX492 flew 57 operational sorties, dropping 12 1,000lb bombs and one confirmed Skyhawk kill. D/D 19.7.82 to 899 coded 712, the 800 30.7.87 coded 128. Back to 899 89 coded 713 then 801 coded 002. To conversion 8.1.94.

XZ493 F/F – 26.11.80 (Pilot J. Farley). D/D 6.1.81 at 2:17 A/F hrs to Yeovilton for 801 coded 001. Between 1.5 and 14.6.82 flew 35 sorties with 801 dropping one 1,000lb bomb. D/D 17.9.82 to 800 coded 123, followed by Phase 1 update 1987 and 801 coded 006. D/D 899 coded 714 9.6.93, D/D 801 27.1.94 coded 007 then 800 23.6.94 coded 126. W/O 15.12.94 lost yaw control in hover alongside *Invincible* and ditched – pilot Lt D. Kistruck ejected safely. A/F hours at loss 2684:15.

XZ494 F/F – 24.10.80 (Pilot J. Farley). D/D 5.12.80 to 899 at 4:30 A/F hrs coded 716. Flown by Lt-Cdr Auld the aircraft led the attack on Stanley airfield 1.5.82, dropping cluster bombs. 16.5.82 Lt McHarg dropped two 1,000lb bombs and fired 200 30mm rounds at the *Rio Carcarana*. Flew 52 sorties in area with a shared claim for the ship attack. Transferred on station to 801 4.7.82 coded 008. D/D back to 899 coded 716 15.1.84 Phase 1 update 1986. 19.4.93 to 800 coded 126, then 801 1.2.94 coded 001, now 800 31.5.94 coded 122.

XZ495 F/F – 3.2.81 (Pilot H. Frick). D/D 11.3.81 at 4:25 A/F hrs to 899 then 801 2.4 coded 003. 1.5.82 Lt-Cdr Ward fired 160 rounds 30mm at Mentor damaging canopy. Flew 87 sorties in area dropping six 1,000lb bombs and firing 30mm twice. Stayed with 801 until Phase 1 update 1986, then D/D 13.8.86 to 899 coded 714. 24.6.91 to conversion to FA 2 – delivered FA 2 to 899 OEU 11.10.93 coded 713. W/O 5.1.94 lost in Bristol Channel following engine failure. Pilot Lt Wilson ejected safely.

XZ496 F/F – 9.12.80 (Pilot T. Scott). D/D 11.2.81 at 6:50 A/F hrs coded 002. To St Athan 7.81 and reissued to 800 31.1.81 coded 127. 4.82 recoded 27. 1.5.82 Lt Thomas toss-bombed three 1,000lb bombs onto Stanley airfield. 21.5.82 Lt-Cdr Blissett engaged one Skyhawk with Sidewinder achieving a successful kill. Flew 59 operational sorties with one confirmed kill – Skyhawk. With 800 6.12.82 coded 126 W/O 16.3.84 alongside *Illustrious* due to engine failure – pilot ejected safely. A/F hrs at loss 948:05.

XZ497 F/F – 2.4.82 (Pilot T. Scott). D/D to Yeovilton 22.4.82 at 3:22 A/F hrs. Flown by 809 and 899 coded 4, then returned to BAe 2.8.82 for development flying. Third aircraft converted to FA 2 and D/D 23.3.93 to A&AEE, alternating between the two ever since.

XZ498 F/F – 26.3.81 (Pilot H. Frick). D/D 13.5.81 at 3:20 A/F hrs then to 801 coded 005. Between 1.5.82 and 14.6.82 flew 69 operational sorties with 801, dropping 12 1,000lb bombs and three lepus flares. To 800 coded 124 17.9.82 then last aircraft to leave Yeovilton for Phase 1 update 18.11.87. Back to 801 23.5.88 followed by Aircraft Maintenance Group and 800 coded 124 19.3.94. Transferred to 801 1.2.94 coded 002. W/O 16.4.94 shot down near Gorazde in Bosnia by AAM with pilot Lt N. Richardson ejecting safely. 2881:05 A/F hrs at loss.

XZ499 F/F – 12.6.81 (Pilot T. Scott). D/D at 3:19 A/F to 801 22.7.81 coded 002. Recoded 000 9.81. To 809 15.4.82 flown south by Lt-Cdr Craig to Banjul, Gambia then on to *Atlantic Conveyor* at Ascension. 18.5.82 transferred to *Hermes* and 800 by Flt Lt Leeming, coded 99. 21.5.82 Lt Hale fired Sidewinder at Dagger, although missile exploded short. 22.5.82 Lt Hale strafed the patrol boat *Rio Iguaza* causing it to beach. 8.6.82 Lt-Cdr Smith engaged and destroyed a Skyhawk with Sidewinder. Total record during conflict – flew 38 sorties, firing two AIM-9L Sidewinders, destroying one Skyhawk. 19.7.82 returned to 809 coded 255 returning to 801 6.12.82. 29.10.85 to 800 coded 126. Take-off accident Oct 86 during heavy weather carrier launch off Australia. Outrigger torn off in ramp netting – pilot Lt Miskin recovered safely by landing aircraft normally and resting on wingtip. Phase 1 update 23.3.87 then 899 11.9.87 coded 715. D/D 20.8.90 to 801 coded 001, then 800 28.2.94 coded 123. Loaned to 801 7.94 for short period, now back with 800.

XZ500 F/F – 28.5.81 (Pilot T. Scott). D/D 5.8.81 at 5:06 A/F hrs to 800 26.8.81 coded 128, then 130. 1.5.82 dropped three 1,000lb bombs on Stanley airfield flown by Lt-Cdr Ogilvy. 16.5.82 Lt-Cdr Auld strafed the freighter *Bahia Buen Suceso*, disabling the vessel.

21.5.82 Flt Lt Leeming successfully engaged A4 Skyhawk, experiencing difficulty with Sidewinder acquisition and resorting to a guns attack. Flew 56 operational sorties damaging one ship and one confirmed Skyhawk kill. D/D 19.7.82 to 809 coded 252 returning to 800 6.12.82 coded 127. W/O 15.6.83 in Bay of Biscay after a protracted inverted spin, with pilot Lt Hargreaves ejecting safely.

ZA174 F/F – 15.9.81 (Pilot H. Frick). D/D 16.11.81 to 801 coded 002. Issued to 809 and flown to *Atlantic Conveyor* at Ascension by Lt-Cdr Braithwaite. 19.5.82 Lt-Cdr Craig flies to *Invincible* and 801 coded 000. From 19–29.5.82 flew 22 sorties. W/O 23.5.82 whilst positioning for take-off slipped over side of ship due to deck movement. Pilot Lt-Cdr Broadwater ejected safely.

ZA175 F/F – 28.10.81 (Pilot J. Farley). D/D 7.12.81 to 899 at 4:18 A/F hrs. In use reserve with 899 then 801 coded 004. 1.5.82 Lt-Cdr Broadwater fired two Sidewinder AIM-9Ls at a Canberra causing some damage, but the aircraft returned safely to Argentina. 21.5.82 Lt-Cdr Ward destroyed a Dagger aircraft with Sidewinder. Between 1.5 and 14.6.82 ZA175 flew 91 operational sorties, dropping 16 1,000lb bombs and firing three Sidewinder missiles, obtaining one confirmed Dagger kill and one damaged Canberra. D/D 17.9.82 to 800 coded 127, then 899 16.1.84 coded 710. Stored then reissued to 801 13.5.86 coded 003. Phase 1 update 5.3.87 and back to 899 coded 713. 28.11.91 899 coded 711 then to FA 2 conversion 28.6.94.

ZA176 F/F – 29.1.81 (Pilot J. Farley). Delivered to St Athan 16.12.81 via Yeovilton. To 809 flown south by Lt Austin to *Atlantic Conveyor* at Ascension. 18.5.82 to *Hermes* with Lt Covington. 43 operational sorties of no particular note completed by 14.6.82. Returned for 801 6.12.82 coded 001. 7.6.83 pilot Lt I. Watson caused international incident when landed on Spanish freighter *Alraigo* after NAVHARS failure caused near loss due to lack of fuel. Aircraft returned to UK 21.6.83 on British tanker as deck cargo. Phase 1 update 15.6.87. 19.1.88 to 801 coded 007 then 800 coded 122. Conversion to FA 2 22.10.91 D/D to 899 23.11.93 coded 716. Transferred to 801 6.10.94 coded 000.

ZA177 F/F – 5.12.81 (Pilot M. Snelling). D/D 6.1.82 to St Athan then to 809 8.4.82 flown south to Banjul, Gambia by Lt-Cdr Craig in 6:05 hrs. 18.5.82 flown to *Hermes* and 800 by Lt-Cdr Slade. 1.6. and 8.6.82 was used to lead in a pair of replacement GR3s flown south from Ascension by Flt Lts Leeming and Ball respectively. 8.6.82 Flt Lt Morgan engaged three Skyhawk aircraft downing two with Sidewinder and damaging the third with guns, which was then finished off by Lt Smith in ZX499 with AIM-9L. In total 177 flew 43 sorties, with two confirmed Skyhawk kills and a share in a third. D/D 22.7.82 to 899 coded 711 and W/O 21.1.83 when visiting *Hermes*. Crashed in a spin – A/F hrs at loss 362:55. Pilot Lt Fox ejected suffering spinal injuries.

ZA190 F/F – 5.11.81 (Pilot J. Farley). D/D to Yeovilton 7.12.81 for 809 and flown south by Lt-Cdr T. Gedge. 18.5.82 transferred via *Hermes* to 801 and *Invincible* recoded 009. 21.5.82 Lt Thomas engaged and destroyed two Dagger aircraft with Sidewinder, sustained ground fire on return journey. 23.5.82 Lt-Cdr Braithwaite fired 183 rounds 30mm ammunition sharing in the destruction of a Puma on the ground. In total flew 54 operational sorties, with two confirmed Dagger kills and a share in a Puma. 15.12.82 to St Athan for Battle Damage Repair then 29.6.83 to 801 coded 001. Phase 1 update 2/87 then D/D 25.9.87 to 801 coded 006. W/O 15.10.87 following birdstrike – pilot ejected safely.

ZA191 F/F – 4.12.81 (Pilot H. Frick). D/D to St Athan at 3:25 A/F hrs 5.1.82. Issued to 899 and transferred to 800 2.4.82 recoded 18. 1.5.82 Lt-Cdr Frederiksen led attack on Goose Green airstrip dropping cluster bombs. 9.5.82 Flt Lt Morgan attacked fishing boat *Narwal* with 1,000lb bomb and 200 rounds 30mm. 16.5.82 Lt Hargreaves strafed supply ship *Bahia Buen Suceso* with a further 200 rounds. 23.5 Flt Lt Leeming strafed an A109 helicopter with 200 rounds, sharing in its destruction with Flt Lt Morgan in ZA192. In total flew 71 operational sorties, firing 600 rounds 30mm and sharing destruction of two ships and one helicopter. D/D 899 6.12.82 coded 712 until brake fire in 1983 required visit to maintenance unit. 800 as 123 until Phase 1 update 27.4.87. Issued 14.8.89 to 801 coded 004. W/O 4.10.89 hit *Ark Royal*'s mast during flypast,

damaging wingtip and puffer duct. Pilot Lt P. Simmonds-Short ejected safely over Lyme Bay. 1717:00 A/F hrs at loss.

ZA192 F/F – 29.1.82 (Pilot J. Farley). D/D to Yeovilton 3.3.82 for storage at 3:38 A/F hrs issued to 800 4.4.82 coded 92. 1.5.82 Flt Lt Morgan dropped three cluster bombs on Stanley airfield, suffering a 20mm round through the tail fin but recovering safely to *Hermes* 23.5.82 Flt Lt Morgan was involved in the destruction of three helicopters when a Puma crashed trying to evade him as he strafed another Puma and an A109. Both these credits were shared with other Sea Harriers. W/O after taking-off for 23rd operational sortie with three 1,000lb bombs and exploding, killing the pilot Lt-Cdr Batt. A/F hrs at loss 63:05.

ZA193 F/F – 13.11.82 (Pilot J. Farley). D/D 2.2.82 to St Athan at 2:22 A/F hrs and issued to 800 4.4.82 coded 93. 1.5.82 Lt-Cdr Blissett dropped three cluster bombs on Stanley airfield. 24.5.82 Lt-Cdr Smith successfully destroyed a Dagger with Sidewinder. Flew 61 operational sorties with one confirmed Dagger kill, expending one AIM-9L. Transferred to 801 6.12.82 coded 004 then service with 800 and 801 same side code until Phase 1 update 16.10.85. D/D 16.5.86 to A&AEE for Phase 1 CA release flying. Reissued to 801 1.12.89 then Dec 91 to 800 coded 128 then 126 in May 92. W/O 25.8.92 ditched alongside *Invincible* when forward pitch nozzle control was lost during approach to land. Pilot Lt Wilson ejected safely.

ZA194 F/F – 23.4.82. (Pilot M. Snelling). D/D 28.4.82 to 809 flown south by Flt Lt Brown to Banjul, Gambia, and thence to the *Atlantic Conveyor* at Ascension. 18.5.82 to 800 in *Hermes* coded 94. 23.5.82 Lt Hale shoots down Dagger with Sidewinder AIM-9L. In total flew 33 sorties with one confirmed Dagger kill. Transferred to 809 19.7.82 then 899 coded 716. W/O 20.10.83 after crash following control restriction – pilot Major O'Hara USMC ejected safely. 73:00 A/F hrs at loss.

ZA195 F/F – 9.9.83 (Pilot T. Scott). D/D 25.1.84 at 6:19 A/F hrs to 899 and issued to 899 as 710. This aircraft has been built as a development aircraft to replace XZ438 and XZ450 lost in the South Atlantic. Returned to BAe 24.7.85 for Sea Eagle development and then the

first conversion to FA 2 as DBI. Since return to BAe it has constantly moved between Dunsfold and A&AEE.

ZD578 F/F – 7.3.85 (Pilot H. Frick). D/D 27.3.85 at 2:05 A/F hrs. 899 18.4.85 (711). Phase 1 update 28.10.86. 24.2.87 800 (125). A&AEE 6.10.88. 16.10.89 800 (129). 12.10.90 801 (001). 2.3.92 899 (715). 13.12.93 801 (001). 1.2.94 800 (124). 5.5.94 to FA 2 conversion.

ZD579 D/D 899 20.5.85 at 4:05 A/F hrs coded 710. Phase 1 update 7.11.86. 25.3.87 800 (126). 5.7.88 899 (719). 27.1.89 801 (005). 15.5.89 A&AEE. 9.11.90 800 (124). 8.4.92 801 (001). 2.6.92 800 (126) to replace ZA193. 5.3.93 to FA 2 conversion. 27.8.94 899 (726).

ZD580 D/D 801 10.7.85 at 3:14 A/F coded 004. Phase 1 update 12.12.86. 15.6.87 899 (716). Aircraft Maintenance Group 1988. 28.2.89 899 (714). 11.9.91 800 (122). 21.6.93 899. To FA 2 conversion 27.7.93 at Dunsfold.

ZD581 D/D 899 29.8.85 at 5:58 A/F hrs coded 721. Phase 1 update 30.10.86. 899 recoded 718 26.1.87. 27.7.90 still 718. 19.11.92 801 (000). 20.8.93 800 (124).

ZD582 D/D to 800 7.10.85 at 5:20 A/F hrs coded 124. 22.1.87 Phase 1 update. 28.5.87 800 (127). 1.2.90 801 (002). 22.7.91 to conversion into FA 2. 5.1.94 899 (710).

ZD607 D/D to 899 at 6:13 A/F hrs coded 712 on 6.11.85. Phase 1 update 3.12.86. 24.11.87 800 (123). 9.6.88 801 (006). 6.9.89 St Athan. 2.3.90 800 (127). 15.7.92 899. 12.8.92 801 (001). 29.7.93 800. 31.5.94 801 (001). 23.9.94 to conversion into FA 2 at Dunsfold.

ZD608 D/D to St Athan at 4:49 A/F hrs for Phase 1 update and storage 17.10.85. 22.11.86 801 (000). 27.10.88 899 (710). 19.4.91 801 (000). 18.11.92 to conversion into FA 2 at Dunsfold. 3.8.94. 899 (717).

ZD609 F/F – 19.10.85 (Pilot Hopkins). D/D 800 11.12.85 at 2:30 A/F hrs. 11.12.85 800 (123). Recoded 122 24.3.86. 1.5.86 flown from Yeovilton to Pensacola, Florida to take part in the 75th USN Anniversary air show. 10.5.86 aircraft landed wheels-up at beginning of show, brought home on RFA *Reliant*. Phase 1 update late 86. 27.5.88 801 (000). 7.12.90 801 (006). W/O 10.5.91 crashed in South Wales following control restriction. Pilot Lt H. Mitchell ejected with serious injuries. 1066:10 A/F hrs at loss.

ZD610 D/D St Athan 11.12.85 for storage and Phase 1 update at 3:40 A/F hrs. 30.1.87 899 (711). 22.2.90 899 (713). 2.9.92 899 (710). 3.11.93 801 (004). 16.9.94 900 (004). 29.9.94 800 (129). Last Sea Harrier FRS 1 to leave Yeovilton for front line service.

ZD611 D/D to St Athan 11.12.85 for Phase 1 update at 3:16 A/F hrs. 25.11.86 801 (001). 7.11.88 899 (717). 15.11.90 800 (123). 9.1.91 801 (123). 12.1.91 800 (123). 24.3.93 for conversion to FA 2. 23.9.94 899 (716).

ZD612 D/D St Athan 9.1.86 at 4:38 A/F hrs. 6.3.86 Phase 1 update. 29.8.86 899 (711). 7.1.87 801 (002). 18.6.90 800 (128). 18.12.91 to conversion to FA 2. 9.2.94 899 (724).

ZD613 D/D St Athan at 6:35 A/F hrs for Phase 1 update. 4.11.86 899 (710). 14.3.89 801 (003). Recoded 000 16.7.90. 15.10.91 899 (712). 31.7.92 A&AEE (712). 25.8.92 899 (712). 26.6.93 to St Athan then Dunsfold for conversion to FA 2. 3.11.94 801 (005).

ZD614 F/F – 14.3.86 (Pilot Hopkins). D/D 7.4.86 for Phase 1 update. 26.1.87 800 (124). 22.9.89 800 (125). 19.3.92 801 (004). 29.7.93 800. 22.6.94 802 (002). 26.9.94 800

(128). 9.12.94 to St Athan and Dunsfold for conversion to FA 2.

ZD615 D/D 19.6.86 to St Athan for Phase 1 update. 3.12.86 801 (005). 15.5.89 800 (124). 14.11.90 for conversion to FA2 at Dunsfold. First FA 2 to 899 OEU 18.8.93 (723).

ALL THE 'ZE' BATCH AIRCRAFT WERE BUILT WITH THE PHASE ONE UPDATE INCORPORATED.

ZE690 D/D 13.11.87 to St Athan for storage. 1.5.91 899 (711) at 16:55 A/F hrs when received. 8.2.93 899 (711). Dunsfold 25.2.93 for FA 2 conversion. 18.5.94 899. 20.10.94 801 (003).

ZE691 D/D to St Athan 23.11.87 for storage. 13.8.91 at 11:25 A/F hrs to 800 (124). 11.1.93 801 (006). 4.2.93 899 (006). 2.6.93 to Dunsfold for FA 2 conversion.

ZE692 D/D to St Athan 8.12.87 for storage. 11.12.91 at 7:10 A/F hrs to 899 (713). 19.1.93 801 (005). 2.3.94 to Dunsfold for conversion.

ZE693 D/D to St Athan 5.1.88 for storage. 7.12.89 801 (005) at 11:25 A/F hrs. 22.1.92 800 (127). 11.1.93 801 (007). 19.2.93 800 (127). 24.7.94 801 (003). 22.8.94 BAe FA 2 conversion.

ZE694 D/D 8.3.88 to St Athan for storage. At 11:05 A/F hrs 10.4.90 to 800

(126). 12.7.91 800 (126). 6.1.93 801 (003). 16.7.94 800 (125).

ZE695 To St Athan for storage 2.2.88. Not issued to RN as FRS 1 but sent back to BAe to become the second production FA 2 conversion. Issued to 899 coded 711 at 24:45 A/F hrs.

ZE696 D/D Athan 6.4.88 at 2:45 A/F hrs. Issued to 800 26.7.88 (123). 19.10.90 899 717. 6.9.91 801 (001). 6.4.92 for conversion to FA 2. 30.4.94 899 (713).

ZE697 To St Athan 13.5.88 for storage at 6:18 A/F hrs. 6.7.88 800 (122). 7.9.90 899. 18.9.90 800 (123). 22.5.91 801 (005). 28.7.92 for conversion to FA 2. 3.5.94 899 (715).

ZE698 To St Athan for storage 16.8.88 26.2.90 801 (007). 18.9.92 899 (716). 12.11.93 801 (005). 20.8.94 800 (127). Last operational sortie FRS 1 18.2.95, and last front line FRS 1 to depart HMS *Invincible* 25.2.95 for FA 2 conversion.

18 FA 2 new build aircraft are currently under construction at BAe Dunsfold, numbered ZH796 – ZH813.

The following T4 (N) trainers have been used by 899 Naval Air Squadron in the VSTOL training programme.

XW927/XW266/XW267/XW268/XZ445/ ZB603/ZB604/ZB605/ZB606/ZD992.

To mark the passing of the FRS 1 from service, 800 NAS put up the last eight-ship formation during a weapons training period in the Toulon exercise areas. Led by the CO, the diamond runs in over *Invincible* on 27 October 1994.

OVERLEAF:
Over its natural environment, this unusually painted Extra-Dark Sea-Grey FA 2 turns through the glint on the sea at the end of another training sortie from Yeovilton.

ABOVE:
On 18 February 1995, FRS 1 127/ZE698 of 800 NAS flew the last operational Combat Air Support mission of the type over Bosnia. Seen here on the final sortie over the characteristic terrain west of Gornji Vakuf, the Sea Harrier FRS 1 provided over 360 sorties for the United Nations 'Deny Flight' Operations between September 1994 and February 1995, consolidating its position as the premier reliable and flexible fixed-wing asset in theatre.

LEFT:
Serviceability problems with the T4(N) VSTOL trainers have cleared up over the last three years, allowing unique photography such as this four-ship formation, believed to be the first time that all four currently in use have been seen together in the air.